WHOLE TRUTH

WHOLE TRUTH

**A FRESH
MONEY-MAKING
METHOD TO WHOLESALE,
THE MOST
MISUNDERSTOOD
SIDE OF YOUR BUSINESS**

DALE POLLAK

vAuto Press

This publication is designed to provide accurate and authoritative information in regard to the subject matter covered. It is sold with the understanding that the publisher and author are not engaged in rendering legal, accounting, or other professional services. If legal advice or other expert assistance is required, the services of a competent professional should be sought.

Published by V Auto Press
Oakbrook Terrace, IL
www.vauto.com

Distributed by Greenleaf Book Group

For ordering information or special discounts for bulk purchases, please contact Greenleaf Book Group at PO Box 91869, Austin, TX 78709, 512.891.6100.

Design and composition by Greenleaf Book Group
Cover design by Greenleaf Book Group and The MX Group in Burr Ridge, IL. www.themxgroup.com.

Publisher's Cataloging-in-Publication data is available.

Print ISBN: 978-0-9992427-8-0

eBook ISBN: 978-0-9992427-9-7

Part of the Tree Neutral® program, which offsets the number of trees consumed in the production and printing of this book by taking proactive steps, such as planting trees in direct proportion to the number of trees used: www.treeneutral.com

Tree Neutral

Printed in the United States of America on acid-free paper

22 23 24 25 26 27   11 10 9 8 7 6 5 4 3 2

First Edition

This book is dedicated to my father, Len Pollak, who passed away on January 1, 2020. He came up in the car business the old-fashioned way. He sold cars and worked his way up to management. He parlayed this success into owning an auction and an independent used vehicle dealership. Later, he achieved his dream of being a successful new vehicle dealer in northwest Indiana and the Chicago suburbs. This book extends my father's generosity of spirit, his insatiable curiosity about the car business, and his desire to make the business better for everyone.

CONTENTS

Contents

ACKNOWLEDGMENTS

I n the summer of 2020, I felt a little bit like John Belushi's character "Joliet" Jake Blues in *The Blues Brothers*.

I wasn't getting out of prison, and I wasn't putting a band together. But I was assembling a team to help produce what I knew would be a new book and a new solution that would seek to change the way dealers think about wholesaling vehicles. Also, like Joliet Jake, I knew I'd need help from some guys I'd worked with in the past.

The first guy is Chris Stutsman, who I've known and worked with since our time at Digital Motorworks, Inc., in the late 1990s, and later at vAuto. Then, as now, Chris has been instrumental in helping me turn a vision into an actual solution. In some ways, Chris plays the role that Elwood Blues did to his brother Jake in *The Blues Brothers*. He's tall, and he finds ways around and out of obstacles that arise in any development effort.

The second guy is Tom Barg, co-founder of Chicago-based Keys & Kites. Tom's agency specializes in helping get new ideas and businesses off the ground. Years ago, Tom helped crystallize vAuto's value proposition and branding efforts. He played a similar and vital role in distilling how my new team should talk about a new way for dealers to wholesale vehicles.

The third guy is Lance Helgeson, who has served as ghostwriter for my previous books. Over the years, Lance has earned my confidence and trust for his ability to turn my thoughts and words into prose with punch and purpose. He brings rhyme and rhythm to my reason. He's been tireless as we've worked to bring this book to its final form.

I am deeply grateful to several other individuals who said "yes" when I asked them to join my team and our journey—Zach Hallowell, Ben Flusberg, Mark Ader, and Ed Berkowitz from Cox Automotive. This core group is loaded with insight, intellect, and a deep understanding of the history of the wholesale automotive market and its current state. They've spent countless hours in conversation, meetings, and working sessions to help realize my vision for a better way for dealers to wholesale vehicles. I'm indebted to this group for the commitment, guidance, and inspiration they brought our table and their broader teams.

I'd be woefully remiss, and in trouble, if I didn't acknowledge the ever-growing love and support of my wife, Nancy, and our family. Nancy is the most positive force of nature I have ever known. She's the great woman who makes me a better man and our world a better place. Whatever success I've achieved, I owe to Nancy and my family, who will always be everything to me. I cherish the time Nancy and I share as partners, parents, and now grandparents.

Speaking of invaluable partners, I would be lost without Susan Taft, my executive assistant. I am blessed and grateful for the care, command, discipline, and direction she brings to my day-to-day doings. She's been a godsend to keep me on pace with all the conversations and meetings for this book and the solution it describes, on top of my other duties.

Finally, I'd like to acknowledge all of you who picked up this book. Thank you for your interest and trust. I hope the book helps you chart a new way forward that turns wholesaling vehicles into a consistent source of significant profits for your used vehicle department.

To paraphrase Elwood Blues, "Our Lady of Blessed Acceleration, don't fail us now."

A BOOK OF REVELATION

I t was around Labor Day of 2020 when I knew that I would need to write another book to capture the learnings and lessons I'd gleaned from a deep-dive into the business of wholesaling vehicles. I felt a book would be necessary to help dealers, and the broader wholesale industry, understand how a new method of making money from selling wholesale vehicles had become possible.

The deep-dive followed what amounted to sudden, titanic shifts in the wholesale market itself. As anyone following the car business knows, the wholesale market effectively shut down in the spring of 2020 as the COVID-19 pandemic forced closures and stay-at-home orders across the United States.

Almost overnight, the inventories on dealers' lots lost upwards of 20 percent of their value, according to wholesale valuations from Manheim and others at the time. In such a crisis, many dealers opted to liquidate their inventories in favor of having cash on hand to sustain their businesses in an unprecedented time of uncertainty.

The sudden move to liquidate inventory arrived as physical auctions were shuttered due to COVID-19. As a result, dealers turned to digital auction platforms that remained open to sell vehicles.

Then, almost as quickly, the wholesale market came back to life, albeit with far fewer available vehicles than it would have in a more "normal" year. By the late spring and into the early summer of 2020, retail demand came back surprisingly strong. Dealers who had liquidated inventory now needed to replenish it fast to take advantage of what some termed a retail revival or a retail resurgence.

These market dynamics remain in force as I write in the summer of 2021. Cox Automotive data shows that retail demand for used vehicles is strong, wholesale supplies are running roughly 50 percent below normal level, and dealers are paying well above market averages for wholesale vehicles. At Manheim's digital and physical auctions, transaction prices have climbed above the Manheim Market Report (MMR) averages and remained there longer than they have in the history of the company.

For dealers selling wholesale vehicles in this environment, it's been an unprecedented era of easy money. It's a wholesale market where, as a seller, you can almost do no wrong, even if you try.

These two extremes—from dealers losing significant sums in the wholesale market to making significant money—caught my attention. I thought back to my days as a Cadillac dealer, and how I'd never been blessed with an opportunity to make money every time I wholesaled a vehicle. In fact, like other dealers of my day and even today, I expected to lose money when we sold a wholesale vehicle. And, if we made money, I didn't celebrate. I worried that we'd left money on the table when we traded for the car.

I began to think, and then believe, that the unexpected disruption in the wholesale market was, in fact, Divine Disruption. Market turbulence and volatility combined to teach a lesson to anyone who had the desire, interest, and will to learn it. It felt to me like there might be a big opportunity for dealers, and the broader industry, if we could only figure out what the opportunity might be.

I had a hunch that the market had revealed the possibility that dealers can and should be able to make money when they wholesale vehicles. I began to wonder how this possibility of consistent wholesale profitability might become a reality.

I assembled a team to explore the idea.

The team and I began to study historical wholesale auction data and compare it to recent trends. We were looking to determine whether anyone consistently made money wholesaling vehicles in the years up to the COVID-19 disruption and through it. We found a startling disparity: While some retailers and wholesalers seemed to consistently make money, the story was completely different for most dealers. Week in and week out, year in and year out, dealers seemed to be consistent money-losers in the wholesale market, often contrary to the story their financial statements may have reflected. As a whole, dealers only really made money when wholesale market conditions made it easy or effortless.

We dug deeper. We asked key questions. Why the disparity between dealers and top-performing wholesalers? What are dealers failing to do that others seem to do so well?

We studied the ways dealers decide to wholesale vehicles they don't want to retail, and the hows and whys behind their decisions to sell this inventory through auctions or wholesale buyers. We explored how dealers sell their vehicles, and how their results compare to top-performing wholesalers over time. We examined how dealers account for these decisions on their financial statements, and who and how they hold someone, if anyone, accountable for the decisions. We talked with dealers about how they regard their wholesale investments and the returns they expect. We assessed how the wholesale decisions and selling process affected the retail side of a dealer's used vehicle department.

Against this backdrop, we compared how top-performing wholesalers bring and sell their wholesale vehicles to physical and online auctions. We looked at how they ran their cars, when they ran their cars, and why they ran their cars in specific lanes, at specific times of day.

As the data science and discovery unfolded, it became clear to me that, despite decades in the retail car business, I hadn't really understood what I have come to call the whole truth of wholesaling vehicles.

The team and I found multiple instances where dealers and managers, because they didn't necessarily believe they could or should make money as they sold wholesale vehicles, ran their wholesale operations based on what I would call long-standing half-truths and inefficiencies. These practices, which were essentially the same when I was a dealer, result in suboptimal outcomes and often losses, despite what their financial statements might show.

It didn't take long for me to recognize that, with all the advances in data science and technology, it is, in fact, possible for dealers to make money when they wholesale vehicles rather than leave the money-making to someone else.

With this belief and perspective in mind, the team and I began to envision a solution that might ensure dealers could achieve these more profit-positive outcomes when wholesaling vehicles. We began the effort by tossing out what we believed we knew. We took newly available data and data science to model outcomes for top-performers and map a means for dealers to replicate this success if they choose to do so. We began to build a solution, and I began writing this book.

The book may not be a comfortable read for some. It might raise questions about the processes and the people that currently manage and benefit from selling wholesale vehicles at dealerships. The book, and the solution it describes, challenges the way many dealers regard their wholesale investments and the returns they expect. The book most certainly highlights some of the darker, less-savory sides of the wholesale market that many dealers, including me, overlook as they pursue their purpose as automotive retailers.

The book reveals a new way forward for wholesaling vehicles that eliminates the inconsistencies and creative math that often mask the full, profit-draining whole truth of wholesaling vehicles. The book aims to give dealers a more comprehensive, controllable method to achieve wholesale profits month after month, even as they correctly and rightfully execute a "retail-first" strategy. My hope is that the book gives dealers a good reason to think differently about the way they wholesale vehicles today.

The book also does something I've tried to avoid in each of my previous books. The later chapters that introduce and describe a new solution could be viewed as too much like a sales pitch or, more charitably, an advertorial. It's a purposeful choice on my part. The alternative would be telling the whole truth of wholesaling without offering a better way forward. I understand the risks my decision may pose for my reputation.

In the end, I weighed these risks against what I believe the solution can do for the broader good of dealers and the wholesale industry. At the most fundamental level, the solution, and the new way of thinking the book outlines, stands to make the wholesale market a more efficient, transparent, and profitable place for dealers to do business.

As I stated, the book may cause some revealing, uncomfortable moments.

But such is the nature of telling the whole truth about wholesaling. You can't clear the closet of skeletons unless you open the door and pull them out, one by one.

Buckle in and enjoy the read.

CHAPTER 1

HALF-TRUTHS OF WHOLESALE LOSSES AT POLLAK CADILLAC

I'm still kicking myself thinking about that evening, roughly 30 years ago, when a wholesale buyer told me something about my former used vehicle manager, who'd left the dealership for another store a couple weeks earlier.

At the time, I was like a lot of dealers. I didn't mind seeing a wholesale loss on the financials for the used vehicle department unless it was extremely large. If memory serves, I didn't sweat losing around $5,000 to $10,000 a month due to wholesale losses, provided my manager and team were meeting the retail goals I'd established for the department. If we were retailing 40 to 50 vehicles a month and making $2,000 or better as an average front-end gross profit, I considered ongoing wholesale losses to be the cost of doing business.

In this way, I aligned with how all my peers ran their used vehicle departments. As a group, we were generally fine with some wholesale losses, provided they weren't *too* significant. We were reflecting the best practices and guidance that we'd learned from our time at the National Automobile Dealer Association Dealer Academy or elsewhere. We understood that it was unreasonable to think that we would make money when we wholesaled a vehicle that didn't sell as a retail unit. We also believed that if we made more than $150 to $200 when we took a fresh trade-in to auction or sold it to a buyer, we probably missed an opportunity.

I don't recall spending too much time with my managers and team discussing specific wholesale losses. If a loss occurred with a vehicle we'd just taken in on trade, it signaled to me that we'd probably overpaid for the car. Still, I didn't make too much noise when this happened because, like most dealers, I understood that sometimes we had to step up to acquire the trade to seal a deal for a new vehicle.

Similarly, if a wholesale loss occurred on a used vehicle we'd tried to retail for 90 to 120 days in my inventory, I wasn't terribly concerned if we lost money when a manager sold the unit to a buyer or took it to auction. Like many dealers, I understood that such vehicles probably represented a string of misjudgments or mistakes, from the amount we paid to acquire the unit to the potential fact that nobody seemed to want to buy the car from us.

I would ask questions if a loss on a specific vehicle hit $2,000 or $3,000. In those days, that was significant money, perhaps even more so than today. I would ask the manager what happened. Most times, I would get an explanation that, while not terribly satisfying in the moment, made enough sense that I was able to move on.

In all my years as a dealer, there was only one time I took a deeper look into how my managers were wholesaling vehicles. This deeper look did not occur after seeing a sizable loss on my financial statements. In fact, at the time, the used vehicle department seemed to be doing well. We were making our monthly average of 40 to 50 used vehicle sales, and front-end grosses were on target with my expectations.

My deeper look occurred after my manager had gone to another dealership, and I was looking for someone to replace him. To be honest, I was surprised my now former manager had decided to leave. I thought he had been doing a good job and making good money for us. I hadn't heard that the manager was dissatisfied working for me. It seemed odd that one day he showed up for work and told me he was moving on.

My thinking started to change, and I started to wonder more about how we were wholesaling vehicles, when the wholesale buyer showed up, looking to see if we had any cars we might sell.

I told the buyer that we were fine, and that I'd take his number and call him when we had vehicles we were looking to sell—which would probably be sometime after I'd found a new manager. That's when the buyer told me something I'll never forget.

"You know why Joe (not his real name) left, don't you?" he asked.

"I do," I replied. "He told me he found a better opportunity and he felt he had to take it."

"Well, from what I hear," the buyer said, "there's more to the story."

I asked the buyer what he meant, and he said he'd heard that my manager might have been "taking advantage of me and wanted out before I found out."

That evening, after we'd closed the store for the day, I began what remains my first, and only, deep-dive into the wholesale vehicles we generated from my used vehicle department. I pulled all the paperwork for the past several months. I looked at our retail and wholesale transactions. It didn't take me long to find evidence that suggested that what the buyer had essentially whispered in my ear might well have been true.

After several evenings of studying the wholesale transactions, I started to see a pattern. Inevitably, I'd find instances where several cars went to a single buyer. Among the cars, some transactions would show a loss, while others seemed like we'd been paid more than we should have. To my dismay, this pattern seemed to repeat itself, month after month, as I looked back at the deals my former manager had made in the years he had worked for me.

Not surprisingly, the wholesale transaction losses and apparent overpayments rarely went beyond the realm of a reasonable explanation. It was a $300 loss here, a $500 overpayment there, and so on.

When I compared the transactions to the financial statements, the latter didn't reveal what I came to understand as the manager's shell game. If we showed a wholesale loss on the statement, it never amounted to enough to get my attention. Meanwhile, in the details of the wholesale deals, I began to see the "story" the buyer had alluded to.

I didn't have the heart or stomach to fully calculate how much money the manager had cost my dealership. Once I realized that, through the years, the shell game had cost me well over six figures, I knew I had put my trust in a guy who was basically a flim-flam artist.

Suddenly, the times that I had noticed my manager sitting with the same buyer(s) around his desk began to mean something different. I wondered how many times those meetings ended up with a win-win for the manager and buyer, while I was unnecessarily losing money and didn't know it. I also began to wonder how much of the manager's new house, which he'd had purchased about a year earlier and talked about proudly, had come at the expense of my dealership and trust.

My deeper look also made me think beyond the vehicles we routinely sold to buyers. I now had suspicions about the units we took to auction, too. My review didn't suggest that the auction transactions were necessarily bad or good from a financial perspective. But I couldn't help but wonder how many vehicles that I *thought* were headed to auction ended up someplace else, in someone else's hands in exchange for something that went into my former manager's hands.

I haven't shared this story in a public fashion before. Frankly, it's embarrassing. I considered myself an astute dealer-operator, and I had found evidence, albeit circumstantial, that I wasn't the steward of my family's fortune and store I had thought myself to be. Even worse, I didn't have any real recourse. The manager had moved on, and his sins, which now seemed glaring and obvious, carried enough plausible deniability that I was left to lick my wounds.

I'm sharing this story because it highlights what I've come to understand as the half-truths of wholesale losses. I learned the hard way that the process of wholesaling vehicles, and accounting for these transactions on my dealership's financial statements, only told part of the whole truth about this facet of my business.

My experience also underscores a problem that, based on more recent conversations with dealers, remains hidden and hasn't gone away in all the years that have passed since I was a dealer. Like me, dealers today still pay used vehicle managers on the gross profit the used vehicle department generates, which can create an incentive, or at least a temptation, for managers to get creative about how they dispose of vehicles in the wholesale market. Perhaps the worst part of the problem is that it's happening at a time when dealers across the country need to make all the money they can—and should—in their used vehicle departments.

It is for all these reasons that I believe the time has come for dealers to take a different view of wholesale losses and begin to regard the process of wholesaling vehicles as a source of potential profit—not just an aspect of their businesses where losses are OK and sometimes even welcome.

As I've studied the wholesale market in recent months, it's become clear to me that making money from wholesaling vehicles is not only possible, but it should be a preferred way of doing business for every dealer. The process itself should be more open and transparent, with more accountability and less gamesmanship on the part of managers and others involved in the process.

But this view runs contrary to another belief about wholesaling vehicles. Not only do many dealers believe that it's OK to lose money wholesaling vehicles, but they also believe that they *shouldn't* make money in the wholesale market and, if they do, it's a problem.

Therein lies another half-truth about wholesaling vehicles. While dealers and managers may believe they shouldn't make a profit when they wholesale vehicles, they don't seem to mind when market conditions converge to make wholesale profits easy.

That's what happened in the COVID-19-affected spring and summer of 2020 and into 2021. Let's take a quick look back to help solidify the idea that it's OK to make money wholesaling vehicles from your used vehicle department.

CHAPTER 2

EASY MONEY IN THE WHOLESALE MARKET

Dealers enjoyed a dual blessing in used vehicles from late spring to late summer in 2020.

Despite the COVID-19 pandemic and other head-line-making disruptions, dealers were blessed with strong retail demand. Across the country, dealers set sales and profit records in June, July, and August. For some, the good tidings even rolled into September.

You can see this retail blessing in the National Automobile Dealers Association (NADA) Dealership Financial Profile data. In April, the month when dealers felt the full effects of COVID-related closures that started in March, NADA reports the average net profit per used vehicle hit -$253. This low point primarily resulted from dramatic value reductions in the wholesale values of vehicles. The unprecedented market conditions meant that many cars in dealer inventories were "upside down." Dealers were forced to reckon with cars they now owned for too much money.

But then the tide began to turn. By the end of June, dealers were retailing cars again and making good money. NADA's financial profile data reports the average net profit per used vehicle retailed hit $106 in June. In July, things got even better, with dealers continuing to retail nearly every vehicle they put on their lots. The average retail net profit per used vehicle retailed shot up to $251, according to NADA.

The positive storyline continued into August, with strong retail sales and an average net profit per used vehicle retailed of $344, according to NADA financial profile data.

My conversations with dealers during this time were remarkable. None of us expected, nor had we ever seen such retail resilience. Time and time again, dealers would tell me if they could just get more inventory and find a way to get it for less money, they'd be doing even better.

The second blessing that dealers enjoyed during this time period in 2020 came in the wholesale market.

After an unprecedented drop in wholesale values in March and April, the wholesale market came back to life. Inventory wasn't as plentiful as it had been prior to the pandemic, a fact that caused wholesale values to appreciate through late spring and early summer—and largely through the end of the year.

To be sure, the higher cost of wholesale inventory created a challenge for dealers looking to replenish their lots. But as wholesale values appreciated in late spring and summer, dealers gained another blessing—it was easy to make money when you wholesaled the cars you'd taken in on trade and chose not to retail. We even saw instances where dealers took 90-day-old retail units to auction and made money.

I can't recall a time in my retail automotive career when dealer conversations consistently turned to the subject of making money as dealers wholesaled cars. In more normal market conditions, when wholesale values tended to depreciate over time, dealers would often bemoan the red ink that resulted from sending vehicles to auctions and buyers. If the loss was significant enough, some dealers might even take a deeper look to see what happened and what they might have done better.

But in 2020, making money in wholesale was easy. Dealers noted that they could step up on a trade-in, knowing they'd wholesale the car and get the money they expected, and often a little more, when the vehicle sold.

Comments like "We made $20,000 in wholesale this month" or "We made out like bandits at the auction" were common.

As I'm writing in the summer of 2021, it appears that we are seeing another replay of spring 2020, when it was easy to make money in the wholesale market. Data from Cox Automotive's Manheim auctions shows that vehicles are transacting well above Manheim Market Report average.

But let's stay focused on the fact at hand: The extremes of 2020 and much of 2021 in the wholesale market should serve as a pleasant wake-up call for dealers that they can, and should, regard the wholesale market as something more than just a place where they take cars to lose money or, at best, break even.

I say this because the near-universal experience of dealers making money as they wholesaled vehicles in 2020 and 2021 reveals an important fact about the wholesale market that dealers traditionally don't think about: Every time a vehicle gets sold to a wholesale buyer or at auction, someone is making money.

Historically, dealers have left the money-making to wholesalers. That's because, as retailers, dealers are rightfully focused on retailing cars and maximizing the money-making opportunities the retail market offers. Dealers also tend to believe that if you want to make money in the wholesale market, you need deep experience and expertise to do so. You need to know how much to pay for a wholesale vehicle to acquire, and you need to know, or be able to find, another wholesale outlet where you can sell the vehicle and make money.

But the experiences of 2020 and 2021 suggest that, perhaps, the ability to acquire a vehicle from a customer at a wholesale price and then resell the vehicle in the wholesale market to make money should no longer be the sole province of the wholesalers who have traditionally made this their business. I've come to this conclusion for two reasons.

The first is that, as I mentioned in the introduction, the wholesale market extremes we experienced in 2020 spurred a much deeper look into how the wholesale market works and why some wholesale sellers—whether they're dealers, larger used vehicle retailers, or wholesalers—have been able to make money wholesaling vehicles when the market is less extreme and more normal.

The second reason is that this examination of the wholesale market and seller best practices has led to a new breed of technology and tools that enables dealers to take advantage of the money-making opportunities in the wholesale market, irrespective of how the market moves. Dealers now have a choice to leave the money-making in wholesale vehicles to someone else or keep it for themselves.

This is a significant step forward for the wholesale market and an unprecedented opportunity for dealers who are willing to believe that sizable wholesale and retail profits can co-exist—and even benefit one another—in a used vehicle department that proudly flies a "retail-first" flag and operates accordingly.

When I was a dealer, I never would have considered my used vehicle department to be anything other than a retail-focused operation that, from one month to the next, regarded wholesale losses as a cost of doing business. Today, I'm excited to share how dealers can turn their used vehicle departments into double-barreled businesses, where the profits flow from the retail and wholesale markets, and wholesale losses are largely gone for good.

But before dealers can begin to consider building a double-barreled business in their used vehicle departments, there must be an examination of the half-truths many dealers and managers believe about selling wholesale vehicles and the manner they account for them. Through a discussion of the half-truths, my hope is that dealers and managers, and anyone reading the book, will begin to see the whole truth of what a profit-producing barrel of wholesale business can look like.

CHAPTER 3

HALF-TRUTHS OF "BREAK EVEN OR LOSE"

E very dealership has what dealers or managers call the "backlot" or the "crow's row" of vehicles.

The backlot reference speaks to where dealers and managers often park wholesale vehicles. They're usually out back, at the farthest end of a dealer's lot. The placement underscores that the cars are destined to be sold in the wholesale market. They are *not* vehicles the dealer plans to sell to retail customers. Hence, they should be separated, so no one will confuse the cars with those a dealer or manager has chosen to retail.

The crow's row label signals how dealers and managers think of the wholesale vehicles: They are cast-offs that dealers or managers don't want. Often the vehicles come into the dealership as trade-ins, and a dealer or manager decides they aren't up to snuff as retail units. The cars are parked out back and left for the crows.

"We view selling wholesale vehicles like taking out the trash," says the manager of a Southeast Toyota dealership. "Once we decide to wholesale a vehicle, we don't think about it too much. Our goal is to get rid of it and move on."

I can relate to the way many dealers and managers regard their wholesale vehicles. I held the same view when I was a dealer. I considered myself a retailer, and I didn't pay much attention to what happened to a vehicle after we decided it wouldn't get retailed.

This backseat view of wholesaling vehicles has a long history. It flows from the earliest days of the franchise dealer system, when the privilege and right of an individual to represent an automotive brand was a proud achievement. In those days, and for much of the history of the car business ever since, dealers have regarded their new vehicle departments as the highest priority of the other departments they oversee.

When I started as a dealer in the early 1980s, my father and I focused the bulk of our attention on our new vehicle department, with the used vehicle department coming in at a close second. The pecking order flipped a few years later when, thanks to some significant changes to Cadillac's design and styling, we had fewer new car customers. Then, I spent more time managing the used vehicle department.

If you were to plot the prioritization of franchise dealership departments today—in the summer of 2021 when new vehicle production has yet to catch up from COVID-19 disruptions— many dealers are spending more attention and time on their used vehicle departments. Some might even be considering how the wholesale market currently offers the prospect of making money as they sell wholesale vehicles.

But even if some dealers are thinking more deeply about selling wholesale vehicles right now, I'd submit that such efforts are more opportunistic, given the current moment. Most dealers and managers still stick to the idea that wholesaling vehicles is a byproduct of their retail operations, not a basis for a business that might drive considerable profits. Dealers and managers believe that if and when you wholesale vehicles, you should expect to lose money or break even.

You don't have to look too far to see and understand why dealers effectively expect to lose money as they sell wholesale vehicles. For decades, the National Automobile Dealers Association (NADA) has counseled dealers that they should expect to lose around $150 for every trade-in they decide to wholesale, or possibly make the same amount in profit, according to former NADA consultants, instructors, and NADA Academy students.

NADA also cautions that if they make more than $150/vehicle for each "immediate" wholesale vehicle sale, the additional profit suggests that dealers are likely missing retail deals, most often in new vehicles, because they aren't putting enough money into their trade-in offers. NADA also rightfully advises dealers that when they wholesale a vehicle they've attempted to retail, they should expect to lose money.

I understand that NADA isn't as strident about teaching dealers that it's OK to break even or lose a little money from the sale of vehicles they take in on trade and choose to wholesale. This more recent view is owed, in part, to the rise of technology and tools that can help dealers properly identify the best financial outcome for a vehicle, whether the opportunity exists in the wholesale or retail market. NADA also recognizes the unnatural wholesale market conditions in 2020 and 2021 when making money was easy—even, in some cases, for dealers who tried to retail cars before they decided to wholesale them.

But I would suggest that the time has arrived for dealers and managers to completely and fully let go of the notion that the best they should expect from selling wholesale vehicles is to lose a little money or break even. I say this because I've come to understand something that eluded me the entire time I was a dealer: If you believe the best you can do when you wholesale vehicles is to lose money or break even, then that's the only outcome you'll ever expect to see from your wholesale operations.

What if, for example, you adopted a view that every whole-sale vehicle isn't "trash" that needs to be disposed of and forgotten? What if you held the view that every wholesale vehicle represents an investment of a dealer's money and, by definition, warrants at least a conscious effort to try to turn the investment into a profit?

If dealers and managers begin to believe that wholesaling vehicles rightfully should be a money-making opportunity, this will serve as a welcome beginning to the end of other half-truths about selling wholesale vehicles that lead to less-than-optimal outcomes every time a dealer or manager sells a wholesale vehicle.

Let's have a look at how such half-truths reveal themselves almost every time a dealer asks a manager about how they did when they cleared out the backlot or crow's row of cars and sold them to wholesale buyers or took them to auction.

CHAPTER 4

THE HALF-TRUTH OF "WE GOT THEM ALL SOLD!"

I t's not uncommon for dealers to ask a manager about the vehicles they sold to buyers or took to auction in a month.

It's also not uncommon for managers to respond with something like "We got them all sold!"

But the response, which may be true, doesn't necessarily reflect the whole truth of how effectively and efficiently the manager sold the vehicles, and whether the manager could have done a better job managing the dealer's money invested in the cars.

Half-Truths of Hand-Selling to Buyers

A longtime wholesaler remembers how he first became interested in the wholesale side of the car business.

At the time, nearly 50 years ago, the wholesaler worked as a retail sales associate for one of the larger dealerships in the Northeast. In this role, he'd work directly with customers to determine what the store would pay for a trade-in.

He recalls how there would be some trade-ins he looked forward to the opportunity to sell to a retail customer. He knew he'd acquired the vehicle favorably for the dealer, and he knew, if he had the good fortune to put a customer on the car as a retail unit, he'd be looking at a sizable front-end gross profit.

But then a guy driving a pink Cadillac and wearing a cowboy hat would show up.

"I'm just a little child. I'm barely 20 years old. I'm watching, and I'm trying to pay attention," the wholesaler recounts. "As I'm doing that, this cat drove up in a pink El Dorado convertible and bought the car that I just traded for two seconds ago. The car disappears and it's gone. It was bought only after a two-minute conversation with the manager in the office with the door closed.

"I'm saying, 'holy shit, I could have sold that car for more money. But it's already gone.'"

The wholesaler doesn't know what happened to the car. But from that moment forward, he started to notice the guy in the pink Cadillac came around fairly often, and cars tended to disappear soon after the visit. "He wasn't the guy selling polyester suits out of his trunk," he says. "That was a different guy. He was an interesting dude, in and of himself. You just sold a car, and you're buying a $29 suit, Madras in fact, so you could look like every other car salesman in the world. No, the difference is the guy with the Cadillac and cowboy hat was the sharpest guy in the room. Every time he showed up, the manager was dancing to his music."

Herein lies a half-truth of managers saying, "We got them all sold!" after working out a deal on a vehicle, or a package of vehicles, with a wholesale buyer. The manager's enthusiastic response may be covering up a few other truths about the transaction.

One truth is that the wholesaler's offer typically doesn't represent the most money the dealer might receive for the vehicle. Wholesalers understand they offer significant convenience for dealers and managers. They turn unwanted vehicles into quick cash, and dealers pay a premium for the service. As a result, the wholesaler's offer often represents what he/she believes is a number that will afford a sufficient profit

A BIT ABOUT "THE PROGRAM"

When I first heard about "the Program," I needed more details. The wholesaler was a bit coy, but here's what I found out:

At one time, "the Program" apparently represented an understanding among wholesalers that, with some managers in some stores, a certain amount of cash was considered necessary if you wanted to do business.

The wholesaler and manager would negotiate the prices for the cars or a package of cars, and cash would be an additional consideration.

I don't hear dealers complaining about "the Program" today. It may be because, over the years, enough dealers had the same realization as me about my former manager, and they have since paid closer attention to how self-interest can sometimes play a role when managers hand-sell vehicles to wholesale buyers.

as he/she resells the vehicle or consigns the vehicle to someone else. In this way, wholesalers extract value from a dealer's wholesale investments. It's also common for a wholesale buyer who acquires vehicles from dealers to work with another wholesaler who ultimately sells the car at auction for a nice profit.

A related truth is that the dealer often isn't privy to the specific details of the manager's negotiations with the buyer. The dealer may understand that the wholesaler helped the manager get rid of all the vehicles in the "crow's row" at the back of the lot. But the dealer won't know a couple of perfectly fine retail units were part of the negotiated "package" the wholesaler took away.

As I noted earlier, I'm now more fully aware that these half-truths happened with some regularity at my dealership. I still remember when the wholesaler said my former manager had been taking advantage of me, and my disbelief that such a thing could happen.

"Oh, yeah," the wholesaler told me. "It's what some guys in the business call 'the program'" (see sidebar, previous page).

Half-Truths of Selling 'em All at Auctions

It's also not uncommon for managers to proclaim, "We got them all sold!" when they sell wholesale vehicles at an auction.

In many cases, the dealer who hears this proclamation won't ask for details. He/she is satisfied to know that the "trash" is gone.

But the data tells a different story.

We know, for example, that many dealers choose to sell some cars directly to wholesale buyers, while they take others to auctions. Perhaps the biggest reason some cars go to wholesale buyers while others go to auction is that dealers can sell cars as-is to wholesale buyers, while auction buyers tend to prefer more assurances about a vehicle's conditions.

Put another way, dealers and managers often cherry-pick the cars they'll send to auction. It's typically the vehicles with the highest investment value—and the best backstory—that auction buyers ultimately see.

This is the arena where managers may tell their dealers, "We got them all sold!"

If this were truly the case, we'd expect to see dealers taking all wholesale vehicles to auction and selling them the first time they run in the lanes. The data tells us that while dealers do take a sizable share of their wholesale to auctions, they often aren't selling them as efficiently as they could or should.

For example, data from Cox Automotive's Manheim auctions suggests that the first-run sales efficiency rates for dealers—that is, the percentage of cars that sell the first time they hit the auction block—runs close to 50 percent. This means that for every ten cars the manager took to auction in a month, five of them didn't sell the first time they ran.

The data also suggests that, of the vehicles that didn't sell the first time, it takes an average of 12 days for most, but not all, of the remaining vehicles to sell. Manheim data indicates that, even after two or three attempts at resale, dealers often still have vehicles that didn't sell.

Some readers might be thinking, "Hey, wait a minute. My manager says they sold all the cars, and none of them came back to the dealership. What are you talking about?"

In such cases, I would submit, the manager found a way to sell them. It might have meant cutting a deal with a would-be buyer, who submitted the vehicle to a post-sale inspection. There, someone found something amiss, and the transaction that the buyer and manager thought they made turned into a no-sale. It's also possible that the manager found someone else, who probably sensed a seller with a need to sell a car.

Ultimately, you can bet that when the dealer or manager worked out a deal with a buyer to purchase the car, the purchase price probably landed below what the dealer's investment could have achieved if the vehicle had sold when it first hit the auction block.

When I learned that the first-run sales efficiency rate average for dealers, who often brought cherry-picked cars to auction, paled in comparison to the nearly 100 percent performance of top wholesale sellers, I asked the data scientists at Manheim for an explanation. I must be honest. I wasn't surprised by the answer.

It turns out that while it's difficult to pinpoint a precise reason why vehicles don't sell in a particular moment at auction, you can discern why the vehicles fell short by comparing the no-sales to the actual sales of the same vehicles. In most cases, I'm told, the vehicles do not sell unless and until the dealer, or the dealer's representative, lowers the floor, or minimum bid, they require for the vehicle to sell.

In light of these facts about dealers' sales efficiency at auctions, I'm hard-pressed to believe that a manager's proclamation that "We got them all sold!" amounts to much more than a half-truth that purposely masks a less-than-ideal performance at the auction.

Let's consider, for example, what an average 50 percent first-run sales efficiency rate looks like over the course of an entire year.

If a dealer takes ten cars to auction every month, they'd send 120 cars to auction every year. Each year, if 50 percent of the cars didn't sell the first time they ran, you'd have a total of 60 cars that most likely sold for a loss.

If each of these vehicles is worth $7,500, which is the average value of vehicles vAuto dealers tend to wholesale each month, these 60 vehicles would represent $450,000 of a dealer's money that's parked in investments that will generate suboptimal returns.

To be clear, I'm not criticizing dealers or managers who consider these outcomes as par for the course. I believe it's a situation where you can't expect any better until you know better.

By the end of this book, I hope to have made the case that dealers shouldn't simply be satisfied when they ask about their wholesale vehicles and hear "We got them all sold!" from a manager. Inevitably, there's more to the whole truth.

Let's examine another half-truth that relates to how dealers and managers determine how much they should make when they sell wholesale vehicles.

CHAPTER 5

A HALF-TRUTH: "WE GOT MORE THAN MMR!"

Dealers usually feel a sense of satisfaction when they're told, "We got more than MMR!" for a vehicle they sold to a wholesale buyer or at auction.

It's usually a manager who relays this good news. The news is typically offered as a proof point that at least one of the vehicles the manager sold to a wholesale buyer or at an auction earned more than the vehicle's published valuation in the Manheim Market Report (MMR).

But there are two problems with the declaration that effectively render it a half-truth.

The first is that MMR, just like the valuations published by Adesa, Black Book, Kelley Blue Book, NADA, and others, do not represent the value of a single vehicle. These valuations represent a roll-up of recent transactions of wholesale vehicles that may share the same make, model, and other characteristics as your vehicle. In other words, the valuations represent an "average" value for your vehicle, not the value you could or should expect when you sell a wholesale vehicle.

When a dealer or manager says, "We got more than MMR!" for a vehicle, it's like using average life expectancy data to determine how long you'll live.

For example, according to the World Bank's data from 2019, the average life expectancy of men in the United States is 78.5 years; for women, the average is 81.1 years. I don't think any of the men reading this book would look at the 78.5-year average and believe that's when they will leave this great life and move on to whatever's next. The same is undoubtedly true for women. You wouldn't expect to turn 81.1 years of age, and then suddenly pass.

I'll go a step further. I'll bet that every man or woman reading this book believes that they'll live longer than the average, since many of us tend to regard ourselves to be above average in more ways than one.

Yet, for some reason, dealers and managers believe that a third-party valuation, which represents an average of wholesale vehicles similar to the one you just sold, is the amount you should get for a vehicle when it sells in the wholesale market. The illogic of the comparison leads me to believe that when someone says, "We got more than MMR!" for a vehicle, it's a way of diverting attention from the sales of other wholesale vehicles that likely amounted to losses.

The second problem with saying, "We got more than MMR!" for a vehicle is that it masks the usefulness of MMR or other valuations to gauge whether you really are achieving the market average when you sell your wholesale vehicles. We know from data at Cox Automotive's Manheim auctions, for example, that 55 percent of dealers achieve MMR across all vehicles they sell at Manheim auctions. Meanwhile, 45 percent of dealers fall short of MMR for the vehicles they sell.

This performance may not seem so bad on the surface. But let's remember the whole truth of the vehicles dealers typically bring to auctions: The vehicles are usually the ones managers pick to send to auction—the ones that they choose not to sell directly to wholesale buyers. The vehicles sold at auction are the cherries, not the rotten apples.

If you're among the 55 percent of dealers that achieved 100 percent of MMR on the sale of all of the vehicles you took to auction, I'd look to see if this achievement spans *all* of your wholesale vehicles, or just the ones you or a manager chose to take to auction.

Meanwhile, if you fall among the 45 percent of dealers who achieve less than 100 percent of MMR on the vehicles you took to auction, I'd look for ways to do better, especially if the MMR performance only relates to vehicles a manager or someone else picked to sell at the auction.

Consider, for example, that if a manager selects 100 cars to auction every year, with an average value of $10,000, and you're getting 98 percent of MMR, you could be missing out on $200 per car, or $20,000 for the 100 cars, that could and should be yours. The missed opportunity is especially true if the manager selected above-average vehicles to wholesale.

This may not seem like big money to some dealers. Perhaps it's an acceptable loss, given the long-standing view that it's OK to lose money when you sell wholesale vehicles. Maybe the upside isn't worth disrupting the status quo.

But I'd submit that if you're cherry-picking vehicles to bring to auction and they are not achieving the market performance, or 100 percent of MMR, there's room for improvement.

I'd also suggest that the starting point for your improvement might come from following the principles of the playbook that top-performing wholesale sellers use to consistently meet or beat market averages. The examination should offer practical ways to improve the proceeds from your wholesale sales and measure your efforts against market averages.

Whatever the case, it's worth investigating if the declaration of "We got more than MMR!" holds true or if it amounts to a half-truth about the success of your wholesaling efforts. I would add that this investigation will need to go deeper than just a review of the wholesale profit/loss line on your financial statements and vehicle logs. I say this because of the half-truths that often hide the whole truth of your wholesale business and its accounting.

CHAPTER 6

HALF-TRUTHS IN YOUR WHOLESALE ACCOUNTING

When you combine a willingness to lose money or break even when you sell wholesale vehicles with the discretion and latitude afforded to managers who keep the books, it can be difficult to get the whole truth of your wholesale business from the financial statements.

More specifically, if you look at the wholesale profit/loss line, it may tell an honest, transparent story. Or it might only tell the story a manager wants the dealer to see.

I've come to understand that the wholesale profit/loss line often tells less-than-honest stories that effectively hide the whole truth of your wholesaling operations. The profit or loss that appears on the statement may look OK, but it isn't necessarily a true reflection of how well the dealer's investment in wholesale vehicles performed in the market.

Consider, for example, tactics managers can apply as they sell and account for wholesale vehicles on the financial statement.

Packaging vehicles. The "packages" combine what might be perfectly good retail units with vehicles the dealership owns for more money than the wholesale market is willing to pay. The outcome? The size of the wholesale loss isn't quite as severe as it would have been if the winners/losers hadn't been packaged together.

Timing wholesale vehicle sales. As most readers likely know, managers are often paid off the gross profit the used vehicle department generates. Hence, there's at least a risk, if not an incentive, for managers to wholesale vehicles they know will result in retail losses. Maybe they overpaid for the car, or it's the wrong car for their market. No one keeps track of what the wholesale market might bring for a vehicle at the time of acquisition. Hence, managers have wiggle room to decide when they want to wholesale

A MANAGER'S POSSIBLE MOTIVATION

Every day, in dealerships across America, used vehicle managers effectively get the shaft.

The shaft comes in the form of trade-in units that were acquired for too much money to sell a new vehicle. Managers look at these cars and wag their heads. They know the car's cost position will make it impossible to make a small, if any, retail gross profit. Meanwhile, the manager's colleagues in the new vehicle department are high-fiving each other. Their side of the deal has more commissionable gross profit. They aren't thinking at all about how their "win" came at the expense of the used vehicle department.

The practice of over-allowing on trade-ins—and charging the cost to the used vehicle department—strikes me as one potential reason managers feel compelled to apply questionable tactics as they wholesale vehicles and account for them on the financial statement. The thinking may go something like this: If the dealer doesn't care that vehicles. The outcome? The financial statement won't reveal the severity of the losses, nor will it say much, if anything, about the opportunity cost of the capital tied up in vehicles that were purposefully set aside.

Working the numbers. I discovered this tactic after my manager had left the dealership, and I heard he might have been a less-than-honest steward. In reviewing the wholesale log, I noticed journal entries that included write-downs of the cost of one vehicle against another. The outcome? The financial statement showed the small loss or profit I expected.

The list of such tactics is as long and wide as a dealer's inventory and the pool of people who manage the dealership's wholesaling efforts. In the end, I would submit that the wholesale profit/loss line on the financial statement is the least accurate and reliable line item on the

I'm constantly taking it on the chin for the new car department and I can get fired for wholesale losses on these cars, then it's only fair for me to look out for myself when I'm wholesaling cars.

I'm not suggesting dealers shouldn't over-allow on trade-ins. Sometimes it's the right and only thing to do. But I do believe the accounting behind these decisions should be more equitable and honest for the used vehicle department.

It seems to me the proper place to account for the over-allowance cost is in the "trade allowance" for the new vehicle deal.

I realize my position, which I outline in Chapter 20, runs counter to tradition. I know that, for many dealers, their new car department comes first. Its primacy is a priority.

But, as dealers look to build a double-barreled business in their used vehicle department, it's essential that the Actual Cash Value (ACV) assigned to the used vehicle represents the actual cash value of the car, not an amount that's engineered to make the new vehicle deal more profitable.

entire statement. It's like the term my musician friend applies to his annual tax filing—"a work of fiction."

At some level, one must ask: Why would someone apply these tactics in the first place? Shouldn't they be earning enough respect and making enough money to do the right thing for the dealer and his/her investment? I don't have answers, but I can think of one reason that may provide motivation (see sidebar, previous page).

Ultimately, if the circumstances outlined in this chapter are in play at a dealership, the whole truth of a dealer's wholesale operations isn't getting told. Dealers who only look to the wholesale profit/loss line on the financial statement to see if they lost a little money or broke even won't see the bigger picture. They don't know if the profit or loss that shows on the line represents an acceptable return on their investments in wholesale vehicles compared to the overall market, or something far different.

Let's say the wholesale profit/loss line shows a $5,000 profit or a $5,000 loss. Most dealers today would simply see that number and move on. They wouldn't consider whether the $5,000 profit should have been $15,000 based on relevant market benchmarks for the vehicles they sold. Similarly, if it's a $5,000 loss, dealers don't know whether the loss represents what the market delivered for the vehicles or the outcome of some creative wholesaling accounting and disposition tactics.

Herein lies a big opportunity for dealers.

The opportunity begins by believing that you can and should make a profit from wholesaling vehicles. The half-truths I've described in this and prior chapters ought to serve as a signal that, in most dealerships, there's considerable room for sizable improvement in their wholesale operations.

In fact, some dealers and managers have made a conscious effort to better understand the whole truth of how they wholesale vehicles and improve the outcomes when they sell wholesale vehicles. It's worth taking a closer look at these attempts to drive more wholesale profits and how they often fall short of the mark.

CHAPTER 7

A JOURNEY TO IMPROVE WHOLESALE OUTCOMES

I f you examine how individual dealers and dealer groups have worked to understand the whole truth of their wholesaling operations, you'll find they often embark on a similar journey.

This journey often starts with a nagging sense and, later, a growing belief that they could get more for the cars they wholesale if they really tried. The thought might even keep some dealers and managers up at night, especially near the end of a month, when they calculate how wholesale losses will hit the used vehicle department's financial statement and paychecks.

When this moment occurs, wholesalers often end up in the crosshairs.

I had a similar moment when I was a Cadillac dealer. It occurred after the wholesaler whispered in my ear about my former used vehicle manager. When I realized that he was probably part of the "program" mentioned in Chapter 4, I understood that the practice of a manager selling vehicles to wholesale buyers brought a level of temptation and risk to my money. I developed what might medically be described as a "latent distrust" for the wholesalers who came to my dealership week in and week out.

I'll confess. I didn't do anything to change this situation, other than hire a new used vehicle manager who I believed would have, and hold, my best interests as his dealer and boss at heart. Just like I did with the guy he replaced.

But some dealers take the next step on the journey. They decide that the days of managers hand-selling vehicles to individual wholesalers has passed. They begin requiring wholesalers to submit sealed bids for their wholesale vehicles. They believe sealed bids might spur more higher bids from buyers in the sealed envelope, and they'll get more for their vehicles.

Broadly speaking, you can't argue with this approach. On the surface, sealed bids should spur buyers to offer a little more, or even as much, as they would for a vehicle if they're negotiating the purchase price of a wholesale vehicle with a dealer or manager. You could make the case that sealed bids get you from Point A to Point B in selling your vehicle a bit faster and more honestly than a dealer and wholesaler hashing out a purchase price—or a package price for several vehicles—can achieve on their own.

Unfortunately, the real world doesn't necessarily work this way.

"I was a wholesaler. I went to the bid sales," says a former wholesaler in the Midwest. "We all talked to each other. I'd tell guys that I'm bidding on this car because I've got a person on it. I'm going to bid it for $12,000. The other guy will bid it for $10,900 so your bid looks good. We rigged it. So, just like anybody would fight for a good deal, that stuff is going on, and the dealers don't know it."

Even with the gamesmanship, dealers and managers are more likely to see better financial outcomes for their wholesale vehicles through a sealed bid auction than hand-selling vehicles directly to wholesalers. Such is the nature of a selling process that moves closer to putting your vehicles in front of a group of potential buyers and bids rather than a single individual.

A second phase of the journey occurs when dealers and managers decide to create their own auctions and use the open bid format and an auctioneer to sell their wholesale vehicles. This step is somewhat more common among dealer groups, where the volume of wholesale vehicles is larger and there's more investment risk on the line.

Dealers and dealer groups will partner with Adesa, Manheim, or another auction provider to run the auctions at or near their dealerships. The auctions often blend in-lane and online sales formats; some are strictly online.

The success of these do-it-yourself-type auctions can be striking compared to the returns dealers and managers realized from sealed bid or direct sales to wholesalers. For example, a six-store dealership group in the Midwest hosts a twice-monthly on-premises auction. The sale sees 50 to 75 buyers, lined up in the lane and online to bid and buy the 100 to 120 vehicles the group puts up for sale. The auction's manager says the operation, which replaced a closed-bid auction, now generates a healthy profit for the dealer.

"The first year, we were knocking on the door of a half-million," the manager says.

The manager agrees that if the vehicles were sold at a larger auction setting and were managed properly, the profitable returns would be even higher. "When there are more buyers, there are more bids," the manager says.

But for all the wholesale turnaround success stories, there are many more instances when dealers attempt to improve the outcomes of their wholesale operations and falter. The efforts often fall victim to some of the same half-truths that plague more conventional approaches to selling wholesale vehicles. The efforts are also typically dependent on one or two individuals who have sufficient wholesaling expertise to find success. If they leave, or take on different responsibilities and roles, the focus on improved wholesale outcomes tends to wane.

Dealers who have tried their hand at improving the outcomes of their wholesale business will appreciate knowing that there is a better way to turn this business into a money-maker, rather than the lose or break-even proposition it represents today. In upcoming chapters, I'll detail a new solution that I believe will help dealers turn their wholesaling operations into a source of significant profits for their used vehicle departments.

My belief in the utility and value of the solution for dealers is buttressed by the fact that some automotive retailers have already demonstrated that selling wholesale vehicles can be a big money-maker. In fact, they now enjoy competitive advantage from building what amounts to a double-barreled business in their used vehicle operations—with profits coming in steady and strong from retail and wholesale vehicle sales.

Let's have a look at two of these double-barreled businesses— both of which are essentially household names and should be familiar to everyone reading this book.

CHAPTER 8

A STUDY IN DOUBLE-BARRELED USED VEHICLE BUSINESSES

When dealers think of CarMax and Carvana, they typically focus on each company's retail operations.

Dealers pay attention to each company's retail operations because each company positions itself as an alternative, better way to buy a car. The implication, of course, is that CarMax and Carvana offer something traditional dealers can't deliver. In this way, the companies compete with every dealer.

CarMax is arguably the first used vehicle retailer to scale the concept of a "no haggle" deal, where the price you see is the price you pay, whether it's the price of the vehicle or the cost/terms of finance and insurance products. The company also found success with another promise: "We'll buy yours even if you don't buy ours."

Carvana is a more recent retail player. They've found favor and financial success with a promise that takes the concept of a "no haggle, no hassle" car deal a step further. Customers don't even have to visit a dealer or showroom in person to get their next used vehicle.

If they prefer, customers can have a vehicle delivered at home or go to one of the company's iconic, glass-tower vending machines to pick up the vehicle they've purchased.

Dealers scratch their heads when they regard Carvana's financials. The company seems to be a darling on Wall Street, and dealers know Carvana is acquiring and selling an increasing number of cars. In some markets, dealers are seeing more customers inquire about trade-ins with a Carvana purchase offer in hand. Even so, dealers, who often have family fortunes on the line as they work month in and month out to make money and payroll, find it difficult to give much credence to an outfit that took years to report a profitable quarter.

But while dealers pay varying degrees of attention to the retailing strategies CarMax and Carvana have taken to market, there's less attention or understanding about each company's respective approach to the process of buying and selling cars in the wholesale market.

The fact is, if you study each company's financials, CarMax and Carvana wouldn't have achieved the level of success they've enjoyed retailing cars, and wooing investors, if they regarded the process of buying and wholesaling cars the same way many of their franchise and independent dealer competitors do.

CarMax and Carvana are arguably the industry's most visible examples of what could be described as double-barreled dealerships.

One barrel represents their retail operations. It's the stuff that gets headlines and makes sense to consumers and investors who, almost to a person, have probably had a vehicle purchase experience at a franchise or independent dealer that they didn't like.

The retail story for both companies has been one of ongoing growth. If you look at what each company has done in just the past three years, it's no wonder dealers are paying attention. If you're a dealer and CarMax and Carvana operate in your vicinity, it's difficult to look at their numbers and wonder how many retail used vehicles could or should have been yours.

In the case of CarMax, the company retailed 671,294 vehicles in fiscal year 2017, reporting $2,163 gross profit average from those sales, according to the company's public financial filings. In fiscal year 2021, which ended February 28, 2021, the company retailed 751,852 vehicles, with a $2,113 gross profit average. The company's performance dipped a bit in fiscal year 2021 due to the impact of the COVID-19 pandemic, but it's otherwise been a story of year-over-year gains in used vehicle sales volume and gross profit.

Meanwhile, Carvana closed 2017, which marked the same year the company went public, with retail sales of 44,252 vehicles and an average gross profit of $741, according to public financial filings. In fiscal year 2020, which ended December 31, 2020, the company retailed 244,111 vehicles, with a gross profit average of $1,472. Those figures represent more than 470 percent growth in retail sales volume, and a nearly 100 percent increase in average gross profit.

Wow. That's impressive.

Now, let's look at the second barrel of each company's business: their wholesale operations.

In fiscal year 2017, CarMax wholesaled 394,686 vehicles, reporting a $926 gross profit average. In fiscal year 2021, the company wholesaled 426,268 vehicles, with a $993 gross profit average. Between fiscal years 2020 and 2021, the effects of the COVID-19 pandemic caused the number of wholesale vehicles sold to dip, while gross profit on wholesale vehicles improved.

Meanwhile, in 2017, Carvana wholesaled 6,509 vehicles, with an average gross profit of $283. By the end of 2020, the company wholesaled 55,204 vehicles, with a $610 average gross profit. In 2020, Carvana also noted two milestones—the company achieved a record in gross profit per unit sold, and it acquired more vehicles directly from customers than it retailed, which resulted in more than half of retail sales coming from customer-purchased vehicles.

Are you following the trendlines? Whether it's retail or whole-sale, CarMax and Carvana seem to be doing better and better as time goes on, no matter the exit strategy for the vehicles they require. To carry the shotgun analogy a step further, both companies seem to be firing both barrels, and hitting their marks, consistently.

But simply looking at the retail and wholesale financials for CarMax and Carvana doesn't fully capture the power of their respective business models. The fact is, both sides of the business feed each other. One makes the other more resilient and stronger. The relationship is akin to the way the new and used vehicle departments at a well-run franchise dealership work hand-in-hand to optimize a dealer's money-making potential.

You can see the strength of the synergy that a strong wholesale business brings to its retail sibling in the way CarMax and Carvana executives talk about their wholesale operations with analysts.

For example, in August 2020, when Carvana reported its financials for the second quarter, an analyst asked the company's executive team on an earnings call about the increase in retail gross profit per unit. The analyst was curious about the drivers behind the growth, and whether it related to acquisition or pricing dynamics in the market.

Carvana's chief financial officer, Mark Jenkins, took the question. His answer, taken from transcripts of the earnings call, is a textbook example of what a strong wholesale business can mean for retail sales and profits:

> There are definitely some exciting trends in retail GPU. I think the most exciting is that, as I mentioned earlier, in July, we bought more than 100 percent as many cars from customers as we sold to customers . . . I think that's obviously a positive that drives wholesale GPU, that drives incremental retail GPU, because cars that you acquire from customers are typically more profitable than cars that you acquire at auction. We're actually acquiring fewer cars from auction now currently than at any point since early 2018. So I think that generally points to a pretty strong dynamic in retail GPU.

Similarly, in September 2020, when CarMax reported its second-quarter financials for fiscal year 2021, an analyst asked the executive team on an earnings call to clarify why the company's SG&A expenses were expected to increase in the months ahead. In the answers, CarMax chief executive officer Bill Nash gave a nod to how important the company's wholesale business, and their ongoing investments in it, are to its money-making goals. Here's Nash's response from a transcript of the earnings call:

There are some things that we're investing in that will pay benefits in other parts of the business. So, for example, improvements in wholesale may not necessarily drive the leverage on a retail cost per car sold. But it will drive improvement in wholesale, which will drive top-line and bottom-line benefits of the company.

When I look at what CarMax and Carvana have done with their wholesale operations, and I compare it to what I see at traditional dealerships, it's like a tale of two cities.

You can bet that CarMax and Carvana do not look at wholesaling vehicles as a break-even or money-losing proposition the way many dealers do. They don't consider wholesaling vehicles to be akin to taking out the trash. These companies, in fact, understand that one person's trash is another person's treasure. Every day, they're taking the proceeds from these treasures to the bank, again and again.

My purpose in sharing the double-barreled business stories from CarMax and Carvana is to help dealers see the possibility that they, too, might begin to believe that consistent wholesale profits are not only possible, but that they also represent a newfound source of profitability that can help them become more successful retailers.

Some readers may be saying: "Well, of course, CarMax and Carvana make money when they wholesale cars. They've got economies of scale, which I'll never have."

In the past, I'd wholeheartedly agree that the kind of wholesale success companies like CarMax and Carvana have achieved might well be out of reach for many dealers. But I would argue the situation's different today, given the rise of a new solution that effectively helps dealers turn the economies of scale larger operators bring to the market to their advantage.

In subsequent chapters, we'll take a much closer look at the solution that will help dealers build double-barreled businesses in their used vehicle departments. Before we go there, however, it's important for dealers to understand the principles of the whole-sale playbook that companies like CarMax and Carvana, as well as top-performing wholesalers, follow to achieve consistent and significant profits when they sell wholesale vehicles.

No one should be surprised that the wholesale playbook has deep roots. Its principles have been honed and refined by generations of wholesalers who—through standing in lanes, breathing exhaust fumes, and selling their investments—gained an understanding of how best to sell vehicles and make money at wholesale auctions. Over the years, the principles have stood the test of time and the advance of technology. You can bet the principles still apply and work well, even as much of the wholesale market for vehicles has shifted to online auctions.

Perhaps the best starting point for understanding the wholesale playbook relates to how top-performing wholesale sellers regard the money they expect to make when they sell vehicles in the wholesale market. They operate under a belief that every vehicle, if managed properly, can achieve its best wholesale price, an amount that, as you'll see, may or may not relate to the wholesale valuations dealers typically rely on today when they sell wholesale vehicles.

CHAPTER 9

AN INTRODUCTION TO BEST WHOLESALE PRICE

I f you build a double-barreled business in your used vehicle department, you have a distinct advantage.

The advantage comes from knowing what the best financial outcome might be for any vehicle, whether it's a retail or wholesale unit. While both CarMax and Carvana are retailers, first and foremost, their success in the wholesale market owes to their ability to acquire—and then wholesale—vehicles to make a profit.

In this way, both companies operate with a different frame of reference as they acquire inventory compared to many other dealers. While the companies may prefer to acquire retail units and pay up to acquire them, they do not regard wholesale vehicles as anything other than an investment opportunity that can and should produce a profit.

But the biggest difference is how the companies regard the return on investment they expect to receive if they sell the vehicle in the wholesale market. For them, it's not about getting back what they paid for the car. Their respective goals are to achieve what I would call a best wholesale price for the vehicle in the wholesale market.

What is the best wholesale price? I would define the term as the highest amount a vehicle will bring in the wholesale market, calculated using well-established best practices that make up the wholesale playbook. The best wholesale price may be higher or lower than a published third-party valuation for the vehicle—a variance that will depend on the specific characteristics and condition of the vehicle and the circumstances that surround the vehicle's eventual sale in an auction setting.

Here's how a long-time wholesaler describes how a vehicle achieves its best wholesale price at auction: "When a car is in front of motivated, capable and able buyers, with an emergency, an auctioneer counting with a hammer and in 15 seconds there's a new owner. The emergency reveals the best wholesale price that comes from the buyer who can pay more money, and the vehicle won't be worth more in any other circumstance."

A Bit of Best Wholesale Price History

The concept of achieving a best wholesale price for a vehicle has been around a long time. Until now, it's largely been the province of wholesalers who build their businesses on the ability to acquire a vehicle from a dealer or another entity and then sell it for its maximum return on investment at an auction.

Some wholesalers trace the pursuit of best wholesale price to what they consider to be the birthplace and epicenter of the automotive wholesale market: Jerome Avenue in the Bronx, New York.

It was along this once-gritty thoroughfare, which still features all manner of auto body and repair shops, that wholesalers would take vehicles they acquired from dealers and sell them to other buyers and dealers, who'd retail the cars. Some of the bigger players around Jerome Avenue went on to create dealer-only auctions in the Northeast that still operate today.

To be sure, the practices in play among wholesalers as recently as the 1970s and 1980s to achieve best wholesale prices for vehicles were less than honest. As one long-time wholesaler recalls, "There was all kinds of crooked shit going on." You can easily find evidence of what the wholesaler was talking about.

A *New York Times* article from April 1978 by Arnold H. Lubasch highlights federal indictments brought against three wholesalers following a United States Attorney office's investigation into "the widespread pattern and practice of rolling back odometers by used-car wholesalers on Jerome Avenue in the Bronx, one of the major areas of supply for used cars sold in the eastern United States."[1]

The piece states that the odometer rollbacks—what wholesalers still refer to as "clocking cars"—effectively "defrauded thousands of car purchasers in the metropolitan area." According to the article's recap of the indictments, the "rollbacks generally ranged from 20,000 to 50,000 miles."

---

1   Lubasch, Arnold H. "3 Auto Dealers in Bronx Indicted on Charges of Altering Odometers." *New York Times,* April 18, 1978. https://www.nytimes.com/1978/04/18/archives/3-auto-dealers-in-bronx-indicted-on-charges-of-altering-odometers.html.

It's probably obvious to many readers why the rollbacks occurred. When you take miles off a vehicle, the vehicle at least has the appearance of being fresher—and worth more—than it would be if odometers hadn't been altered. The piece cites estimates from the Department of Transportation that a vehicle's value would increase "about $100 for each 10,000 miles removed from the odometer."

"The cars didn't just get reconditioned, they went through a transformation," a long-time wholesaler recalls. "The car that you traded and watched go away went through a time machine. It got younger.

"There wasn't any PDR (paintless dent repair) in those days. If the dealer were to put a car with 80,000 miles through their process, it would be done in three weeks and it would still have 80,000 miles on it. But if you have a hustler that bought the car and had it standing on its feet by that afternoon, and somebody tickled the odometer, it's a totally different car, and everybody's happy as hell. The transformation of vehicles in the wholesale market was the way this world worked. Everyone was doing it from coast to coast. It was an accepted practice."

While we might prefer not to recall the less-than-honest and -transparent ways that wholesalers prepared vehicles for sale in the wholesale market, such practices point to a key element of the wholesale playbook: that is, if you can make a car stand tall, or at least seem to stand tall, you have a better opportunity to achieve the best wholesale price for the vehicle when it sells in the wholesale market.

The early wholesalers relied on their experience and knowledge to understand what a best wholesale price might be for a specific vehicle. From my conversations with wholesalers and related research, the early wholesalers' assessment of best wholesale prices would begin with the "sheets" the auctions published and valuation guides like the Galves Auto Price List, which debuted in the late 1950s from M.C. Galves, a wholesaler who'd started out on Jerome Avenue in the 1920s. Similarly, on the West Coast, dealers and wholesalers had been using valuations from the Kelley Car Company, which began publishing valuations in the 1920s and later became the Kelley Blue Book valuation guide.

As a long-time wholesaler explains: "We understood exactly how Galves came up with their prices. Galves was the book that every single trader referenced. I'd buy a vehicle for a grand over Galves, or a grand under Galves. That is the hum line that was relevant. Then, you look at data you knew from your sales experience and the specifics of a car, and the hum line starts to change a little bit. That's when you go a little deeper in terms of what a vehicle is really worth and what it ain't worth."

I've come to understand that the distinction between a published third-party valuation and the actual value of a specific vehicle—and its potential best wholesale price in an auction—is largely lost among dealers and managers who sell wholesale vehicles today. They'll often regard the third-party valuations as the "number" for their vehicle. They don't necessarily account for the fact that a vehicle's best wholesale price might be higher or lower than the published valuation of the vehicle. The best wholesale price might also be more or less than what dealers paid to acquire the vehicle.

But you can bet that CarMax, Carvana, and others understand these distinctions. That's why they invest significant sums in examining the data they derive from the performance of their vehicles in the wholesale market. Their confidence in knowing the amount they should pay to acquire a vehicle—and the best wholesale prices they might derive from its sale in the wholesale market—comes from the way they curate and manage their wholesale sales efforts. In upcoming chapters, we'll examine how top-performing wholesalers take their cars to auction and the playbook principles they follow to ensure buyers want to bid on and buy their vehicles.

Before we begin that discussion, however, it's important to circle back to third-party wholesale valuations and bring more clarity to the reasons why dealers and managers will often incorrectly regard third-party valuations as the value of a vehicle in front of them. We'll examine how this practice can undermine your ability to build a double-barreled business in your used vehicle department.

CHAPTER 10

HOW BEST WHOLESALE PRICES AND VALUATIONS DIFFER

W e've already discussed why dealers and managers shouldn't regard a third-party wholesale valuation for a vehicle to be the actual value of a car. The valuation represents an average value based on the sales of a lot of other similar vehicles. It's not a definitive value for the car in front of you. Rather, the valuation serves as the "hum line" for what a vehicle might be worth.

But while valuations don't necessarily offer the whole truth of a vehicle's potential sale price in the wholesale market, they can help define the data that can now be used—with the benefit of super-smart data scientists and technology—to predict a vehicle's best wholesale price in the wholesale market.

For example, we know third-party vehicle valuations are often derived from a roll-up of the values of vehicles that recently sold at auctions. From this body of data, the third-party companies can derive valuations across make, model, year, mileage, and—to varying degrees—specific trim levels and equipment.

But the distillation of auction transaction prices and associated vehicles doesn't necessarily tell the whole truth of the wholesale sales. For example, the transaction-based valuations typically do not account for the vehicles that do not sell—vehicles that may be essentially the same and run in the same lanes at the same times as the vehicles that sold.

For example, if the valuation guide shows that ten vehicles of the same make and model sold for $10,000, you might presume the vehicle you're appraising or assessing is a $10,000 car, based on the valuation derived from the auction transactions. This value, however, would not tell you that, in addition to the ten vehicles that sold, there were 80 vehicles of the same make and model that didn't sell. You also wouldn't know that the average final bid for the 80 vehicles that did not sell was $8,000. If you knew about the vehicles that didn't sell and the final bids that didn't win, you might be less inclined to believe that the vehicle in front of you is worth $10,000.

In fact, you could make a compelling case that the best wholesale price of the vehicle is closer to $8,000, not the $10,000 listed in the valuation guide. Such are the distinctions and deeper dives into a fuller view of auction data that enable companies like CarMax, Carvana, and top-performing wholesalers to determine the best wholesale prices their vehicles might achieve when they're sold at auction.

The guides don't tell you who sold the cars in their data sample. On the surface, this might not seem significant. But anyone who's purchased auction vehicles knows that the company, dealer, or other individual who is selling the vehicle makes a difference. A top-tier wholesaler—who follows a practice of disclosing as much as he knows about a vehicle's condition and offers a buy-back guarantee if a buyer isn't happy—believes his reputation, which he's carefully managed over the years, offers a competitive advantage.

"When you're looking at all the auction data, you understand something more. You understand that you can get more for a vehicle than the next guy because of your reputation," the wholesaler says. "If someone is all out on a car, I can still pay a thousand more and get it when I sell. When we get to the block, we get more for those cars because of who we are and how we do business."

Valuation guides also tend to fall short of truly accurate representations of vehicle conditions. To be sure, you can get a valuation for a vehicle that adjusts for its condition report score. But, as buyers who source inventory across a variety of auctions can attest, the reason one vehicle earns a 3.5 condition score compared to another can be distinctly different. Similarly, astute wholesale buyers and sellers know that a vehicle's history is important, and it can affirm and inform whether a condition report score seems acceptable and accurate. This is exactly why some buyers simply won't purchase a wholesale vehicle without a cross-check of CARFAX or AutoCheck to understand a vehicle's specific history.

The good news in all this is that data science and technology are converging on wholesale valuations—to the point where we can mine the totality of auction purchases and no-sales to derive a more accurate and relevant valuation for the vehicle in front of you. From there, it's also becoming possible to predict what the best wholesale price might be for a specific vehicle.

In fact, this is precisely the goal my team and I established for a new solution that we believe can help dealers build a second barrel of profit-producing business in their used vehicle departments. The solution seeks to use each vehicle's best wholesale price to guarantee a minimum profit on every vehicle a dealer chooses to wholesale through the system. We'll discuss the solution in greater depth and detail in subsequent chapters.

Meanwhile, it's important for dealers and managers to understand the limitations—and pitfalls—of using third-party valuations to determine the value of a vehicle in front of you. The valuations are useful, but they are not the be-all-end-all of what the vehicle might be worth when it sells in the wholesale market. The valuations are a starting point for determining what you might pay to acquire a vehicle and what you might expect to get if it sells in the wholesale market.

Top-performing wholesalers like CarMax and Carvana also know that there's another aspect to achieving top dollar for wholesale vehicles that goes beyond a more accurate and clear understanding of vehicle values. They recognize that the *way* vehicles are placed and positioned in the wholesale market—and by whom—can have a profound impact and influence on whether the vehicle will achieve its best wholesale price when it sells.

Such factors are part and parcel of the wholesale playbook that CarMax, Carvana, and top wholesalers follow as they sell vehicles in the wholesale market. The elements of the playbook have been around a long time and, no surprise, they make perfect sense when you understand each element and how it combines with the others to effect a profit-positive outcome when you sell a vehicle at wholesale auctions.

Let's examine the first of these playbook elements, which wholesalers and others believe is essential to achieving the best wholesale prices for vehicles in the wholesale market.

CHAPTER 11

PLAYBOOK ELEMENT 1: A QUEST FOR A CURATED CRITICAL QUANTITY OF CARS AND BUYERS

T here's a reason companies like CarMax and Carvana sell their wholesale vehicles at auctions. They do not hand-sell vehicles to wholesalers the way many dealers do.

The reason these companies prefer auctions is sound. They understand that if you want to achieve best wholesale prices for the vehicles you sell, it's always best to do so when you have a curated critical quantity of cars and buyers. You can tell when there's a critical quantity of cars and buyers gathered at the same auction: The evidence shows in a chain reaction of bids that result in vehicles achieving their best wholesale prices when they sell.

By definition, you can't achieve a critical quantity of cars and buyers—or the best wholesale prices—when you're selling a vehicle or a package of vehicles directly to a wholesale buyer. The wholesaler's offer isn't one of several offers on the vehicle. True, you can negotiate the purchase price of the vehicles, but you're still dealing with a single buyer.

The scenario reflects a statement you'll often hear from used vehicle managers, who'd much rather stock their inventories with trade-ins rather than auction purchases: "With a trade-in, it's just the customer and me. At the auction, it's me against everyone else, and I'll pay more."

From my conversations and research for this book, it's become clear to me that auctions are the best place for dealers to achieve best wholesale prices, provided the auction settings offer a curated critical quantity of cars and buyers.

What Critical Quantity Feels and Looks Like

Every buyer, dealer, or manager who buys wholesale vehicles at auction likely has an auction where they prefer to make purchases. If you ask why they prefer a particular auction, you're likely to get answers that could also be used to describe a favorite fishing hole:

"I always get lucky."

"I never go home empty-handed."

"I can always find at least a couple cars I need."

Such comments reflect how a critical quantity of vehicles and buyers at an auction makes purchasing vehicles a more pleasant, or at least preferred, experience. If you need cars, and you go to an auction where the number of available vehicles and competing buyers doesn't amount to a critical quantity, you can bet there will be a larger share of no-sales and a greater degree of frustration among buyers who expected a better sale. The buyers who came home empty-handed may even catch some flak from a dealer or manager who are anxious for additional inventory.

Top-performing wholesale sellers like CarMax and Carvana know that achieving a critical quantity of cars and buyers at an auction setting requires what might be described as mindful curation. It's not about bringing a bunch of cars to an auction and running them randomly. Top-performing wholesale sellers know that best wholesale prices are more likely to occur when they combine cars that make sense together, which makes it easier for interested buyers to find them and bid. This reality is precisely why Carvana and other companies that offer digital auctions have been actively working to build critical quantities of buyers and cars. The companies know that when they can achieve critical quantity, they might realize the premium returns of 2 percent or more that occur at larger auctions with more cars and buyers.

I spoke with a 35-year veteran of the car business who manages a centralized reconditioning and disposition center for an 11-store group in the Midwest. Prior to his current position, the manager spent several years as a wholesaler. From his time in the lanes, he's realized that dealers and managers often don't understand the concept of a critical quantity of cars and buyers, much less the effort it sometimes takes to ensure critical quantity occurs.

"Dealers will throw their cars in the auction," the manager says. "They call at the end of the day to see how many sold. They might say, 'I don't understand what happened with this car,' or 'we made a lot of money on that one,' but they really weren't involved. They didn't get a pulse of the place. They just turned their cars over to the auction."

Today, the manager oversees an on-site wholesale auction for the dealer group. Before every biweekly sale, the manager considers critical quantity as he plans and preps the dealer group's vehicles, and the buyers he invites, for the sale.

"Sometimes it's obvious," he says. "You don't run a one-year-old Mercedes down where they're running $6,000 cars. There won't be any Mercedes buyers standing there. In St. Louis, there are 1,000 guys at the auction and 12 lanes. You have to know the lane where your car should run. Back in the day, I would literally write lane numbers next to our cars so when they checked in, I knew, if I had a hot rod that everybody would be hot on, it would be a matter of getting it in the lane where three or four guys could fight for it. I knew it needed to be in Lane 1. It isn't rocket science. It comes from repetition."

A long-time wholesaler remembers earlier days of auctions, when specific wholesalers would bring dozens of the same makes/models to auctions—effectively creating the first factory sales before the factories started their own. Sometimes, the wholesale sellers would arrange flights and transportation for out-of-state buyers (known as "horses") to ensure their critical quantity of cars would run in front of a critical quantity of curated buyers.

The wholesaler explains: A critical quantity of curated buyers occurs "when Chrysler dealers from all over New York, New Jersey, Pennsylvania, Delaware, and Maryland came in on a Tuesday to purchase cars. In that arena, there were no consigned cars. It was only one guy's cars. As a result, it was like a very specific market.

There weren't Ford trucks or Cadillacs or other kinds of cars. It wasn't a 'spaghetti-eyes' marketplace where there's no rhyme or reason for vehicles to run together. When you put all these buyers and cars together, the energy would be nuclear."

Some readers might be thinking: How am I supposed to curate a critical quantity of cars and buyers when I'm only taking 15 to 20 cars to the auction every month?

The answer to this question lies in the new solution I'll detail in upcoming chapters. The solution, which will be powered by Cox Automotive, will effectively curate the critical quantity of cars and buyers on behalf of participating dealers. The idea is to give every dealer the same critical quantity mass advantage that, at least as of this book writing, largely rests with top-performing wholesalers who know how to curate cars and buyers and who have sufficient volumes of vehicles to do so.

But this chapter should also help dealers and managers understand that, if they choose to pursue best wholesale prices on their own to build a double-barreled business in their used vehicle departments, they will need to be better stewards of their investments in wholesale vehicles.

You won't achieve best wholesale prices if you're selling vehicles directly to wholesalers; in fact, you're probably enabling the wholesaler to achieve the vehicle's best wholesale price. In addition, dealers and managers should recognize that best wholesale prices won't arrive at auction unless you're at least somewhat attentive to the ways top-performing wholesale sellers use the playbook principle of a curated critical quantity of cars and buyers to their advantage.

Now, let's examine another wholesale playbook principle that helps top-performing wholesale sellers achieve best wholesale prices for their vehicles—how to ensure bidding begins, and ends, in a way that enables the best buyers to successfully purchase your vehicles.

CHAPTER 12

PLAYBOOK ELEMENT 2: NO TOLERANCE FOR NO-SALES AT AUCTIONS

f you've ever been to an auction when buyers are flocking around cars and bids are flying, it's a memorable experience.

If you're a buyer in these hot auction moments, you can't help but raise your hand—particularly if the person next to you outbid you on a car you really wanted. You might even make it a point to outbid this person on the next car, whether you really want the car or not.

Such are the "nuclear" moments at auctions. These moments are the product of human nature. No one wants to feel like a loser, and everyone wants to feel like a winner, sometimes at any price.

These moments are no different than those that happen in casinos. I'm not a gambler, but I've spent enough time in casinos, often as part of attending automotive conferences, to have witnessed the dynamic that occurs when the bells, sirens, and strobe lights go off, and coins start flooding the catch tray when someone wins big on a slot machine. Inevitably, the noise and the winner's excitement draw attention. The winner's bounty will spur someone else to feed a nearby slot machine in search of a similar windfall.

In each of these scenarios, someone wins and someone else doubles down on their efforts to win, even though the chances that they'll win are slim. Yet, as sure as the sun will come up tomorrow, these moments will happen again and again, day in and day out, at every auction and casino.

To a casual observer, the moments may seem random.

But casino operators know exactly when and where big wins should occur. They've done all the data science and math. They understand how rewarding certain players, at specific moments, will spur others to spend more.

The same is true among the top-performing wholesale sellers. They know how to use the movement of cars and bids to build momentum that brings out the emotions of buyers and the best wholesale prices for their vehicles. Like casinos, top wholesale sellers orchestrate outcomes to achieve one of their wholesale playbook priorities—to ensure that every vehicle sells the first time they run them.

The practices the top wholesalers employ reflect what might be described as zero tolerance for no-sales, which they regard as a management failure.

Let's consider a scenario where you're selling your vehicles at an auction. You've got dozens, if not hundreds, of vehicles listed for the sale. You've curated the critical quantity of cars and buyers. The cars start to run. The auctioneer's doing his/her best "rubber baby buggy bumper" chant, but the bids are slow to follow.

For a long-time wholesaler, this is a moment where he knows it's time to "fix that shit."

"I'll sell an $80,000 car for $40,000," he says. "I guarantee you that the next car and the next car and the next car we aren't going to have people standing and watching what we're going to do today. The first punch has been thrown. If I've got to throw 35 punches, I'm going to throw them.

"Let's say you've got a car where the floor is $30,000," the wholesaler adds. "You might start that car at $21,000. But if we've got the right number of cars and buyers, that car will start at $31,000 and sell at $34,500. That same $30,000 car in a different situation and nobody's bidding? I'll put that car in there for $10,000. Now, we're going to find out, of the 413 people at the auction and online, whether they plan to buy or not."

These are the master strokes that sellers who use the wholesale playbook apply when their money is on the line and the need arises to nudge the market—to light the kindling that starts a frenzy of bids to sell their cars the first time they run.

"Once you do that and buyers realize what's happening, they can't take a shit," the long-time wholesaler says. "They can't go get a cup of coffee. They can't answer the phone. You want to know why? Because the Jerry Springer effect took place. Anything can happen here. This dumb ass couldn't sell a $10,000 car, he sent it in for $500, and next thing that $10,000 car brings $11,500. When it touches $9,500, and that's all that we can get to get it sold, we sell it. But I'd buy it again for $10,000. That's the cost of putting blood in the water for piranhas. All you've got to think about are the bubbles in the water."

Two aspects of this example of how to execute the sell-them-the-first-time playbook principles are worth calling out.

The first is that the wholesaler, like other top-performing wholesale sellers, isn't afraid to take a loss on a car. It's a no-fear attitude that comes from an understanding that an occasional loss is a means to a more profitable end. It's a mindset that says that wholesale selling success isn't defined by the sale of a single car or a handful of cars. Success arrives through the cumulative total of wins, draws, and losses that are part and parcel of selling cars at auction. You measure your success by comparing how the returns you achieved for your cars in total compare to the market average. If you're meeting the market average, you've done a good job. If you're beating the market average, you're doing even better.

Some readers may be thinking: Hold on . . . if you're purposely taking a loss on a vehicle, you're not getting the best wholesale price. How does that square up?

It's a reasonable question. The answer, though, rests with the moment the decision occurred. Buyers weren't interested, and they weren't bidding. In that moment, the bid that wins the car *would* represent the vehicle's best wholesale price. Had the moment been more friendly to the seller, the car's best wholesale price, in that moment, would unquestionably be higher.

The second aspect of the seller's execution of the sell-them-all playbook principle that should be noted is this: The seller's no-fear mindset—and willingness to take an occasional loss to achieve a better total outcome—is 180 degrees apart from how most dealers and managers think today.

While dealers and managers are willing to lose money on

wholesale vehicles, they don't like it. Their goal is often to get back at least as much as they paid to own the unit. They typically set the floors on the vehicles they sell to recoup their costs. Dealers also tend to focus on the sale of individual vehicles at auctions, not the totality of all their wholesale sales.

When you combine the aversion to loss with the focus on individual vehicles, versus the cumulative performance of all the vehicles a dealer brings to auction, you end up with dealers selling fewer of their auction vehicles the first time they run compared to top-performing wholesale sellers.

In the wholesale market, sales efficiency rates measure a seller's success at selling vehicles the first time they run. The metric makes good sense. It's a way to account for a seller's ability to execute this important principle of the wholesale playbook.

According to Manheim data, the average sales efficiency rate for dealers runs about 50 percent, which means they sell six vehicles the first time they run, and five end up as no-sales. Of the remaining five vehicles, dealers who choose to rerun the vehicles typically sell them in roughly 12 days—and typically for less money than they would have made if the vehicles sold the first time. Dealers and managers should recognize this dynamic because the sales that occur during the second or third auction runs follow a decision to reduce their seller floors.

How does this performance compare to top-performing wholesale sellers like CarMax and Carvana? Well, these companies consistently achieve sales rates of nearly 100 percent, which means they are selling nearly all of their vehicles the first time they run and achieving the highest best wholesale prices on most, if not all, of the vehicles they sell. A top-performing wholesaler says, "I'd go crazy if my sales efficiency was less than 90 percent. If that's the best I could do, I wouldn't be in business."

I recognize that it might be difficult, or even brain-damaging, for dealers to make peace with the fact that getting less than you'd prefer on some wholesale cars is better than holding out for all the money. It runs against your grain. It's not in your nature. You don't run your business with a portfolio approach. You look to manage every vehicle, one by one, to make a profit.

But the fact is, the data indicates you're far less likely to get best wholesale prices for your vehicles if they don't sell the first time they run. Furthermore, the data points to a problem with the way dealers regard and manage seller floors: If they're always firmly set to recoup your costs on the vehicle, you'll inevitably sell fewer vehicles than you could the first time they run. Ergo, you're effectively ignoring a key principle of the wholesale playbook, which other wholesale sellers use to their advantage. Top-performing wholesale sellers know if they curate a critical quantity of cars to attract a critical quantity of buyers and set the floor prices to ensure every vehicle will get bids and sell, they'll come out ahead.

This long-view-minded approach proved out in the spring of 2020, when the wholesale market took a nosedive most of us had never seen before in our automotive careers. COVID-19 had taken hold of the country. Retail sales effectively stopped. Wholesale values of vehicles declined by as much as 20 percent, almost overnight, according to data from Cox Automotive's Manheim and other auctions.

It was a moment of reckoning many dealers would probably prefer to forget. If you had $1 million in used vehicle inventory on your lot, it was suddenly worth $800,000. The near-instant $200,000 loss became a big problem.

Some dealers, like Vroom, took a proactive tack. The company reasoned that since the market had dropped, and its cars had suffered unavoidable losses in value, the time had come to liquidate their current inventory, and replenish it with vehicles that were effectively under-valued due to the sudden market decline.

It was a moment in the history of the car business where the actual wholesale value of vehicles was anybody's best guess. MMR wasn't a reliable reference, since its valuations were based on data collected over the past 30 days. MMR values didn't capture the more recent and sudden drop in wholesale sales and values.

In this volatile environment, Cox Automotive's Manheim auctions reported that Vroom took nearly 1,000 vehicles to Manheim sales. The company knew that there would be some dealers looking to buy inventory—dealers who had already down-sized their stock in anticipation of a once-in-a-career moment to acquire auction vehicles on the cheap.

I don't have any inside track on what Vroom executives were thinking in this moment. But the subsequent sale of their vehicles at auctions demonstrates the power of a well-executed wholesale playbook—where you bring a critical quantity of cars to auction with every intention of selling each one.

The company put its vehicles on the virtual auction block with what might be regarded as ridiculous and risky floor prices or minimum bid requirements. The seller floors weren't based on

Vroom's cost to own the vehicles. The company understood their costs they paid to own the vehicles were irrelevant in the market of that moment. Vroom set the floor for every vehicle at 50 percent below the current MMR values for the vehicles.

Guess what happened? The company achieved a 90 percent first-run sales efficiency rate, at a time when there were far fewer buyers, and available cars, than normal. All in, the company sold its vehicles for 90 percent of MMR, which meant they lost on some cars and beat the market on others. It was an outcome that offered a sharp contrast to the bloodletting many dealers faced as they sold off inventory at the time.

This example underscores how two elements of the whole-sale playbook—a curated critical quantity of cars and buyers and no tolerance for no-sales—can combine to deliver best wholesale prices and better results for dealers selling wholesale vehicles. It's also an example that proves the wisdom of the way a long-time wholesaler regards the seller floors he sets for his vehicles at auction to ensure they sell.

"The circumstances are different on every car, and the time it runs in the lane, and the car that just ran before it, and the car that's going to run after it," a wholesaler says. "But the point is that with seller floors, when you ask too little, you get too much, and when you ask too much, you get too little."

I like this philosophy because it directly ties to a final principle of the wholesale playbook. In some ways, this third principle over-shadows and may even supersede the others. The principle relates to your reputation as a wholesaler seller and how it can under-cut your ability to achieve the best wholesale prices, even if you brought the best cars to the auction.

CHAPTER 13

PLAYBOOK ELEMENT 3: HOW SELLER REPUTATION AFFECTS WHOLESALE SUCCESS

J ust like dealers and managers tend to have auctions where they prefer to purchase, they often have a preferred list of sellers from whom they'll purchase vehicles.

If a seller's name is on the list, it's often because the buyer has come to trust them. The buyer likely had a positive prior experience with the seller. The buyer might have purchased the seller's cars and found them all to be as good as, if not better than, what the buyer expected. The trust might also flow from a less-than-ideal experience. Perhaps the buyer found the seller's cars to be less than expected, and the seller did the right thing right away.

If a seller's name isn't on the list, it's often because of a buyer's lack of trust based on a bad experience. The buyer might have purchased a vehicle from the seller, and the car wasn't up to snuff. Or, the seller refused to do anything to make the buyer feel comfortable the next

WHOLE TRUTH

time he/she might be looking at the seller's vehicles. The buyer's distrust may also be due to sellers saying "no" too often when the buyer's bids don't meet the seller's minimum bid or floor requirement.

Whatever the case, the best sellers are the ones who end up on the "trusted" list of the most buyers. When sellers are trusted, they get more buyers looking at their cars—and more bids on their cars. As a result, reputation is an important principle in the wholesale playbook. When you combine a curated critical quantity of cars and buyers with a policy of no tolerance for no-sales and a positive reputation, you've got a recipe for delivering the high first-run sales efficiency and low no-sale rates that sellers like CarMax, Carvana, and others use to build a double-barreled business in their used vehicle departments.

If you think about it, the reputation of sellers in the wholesale market is no different than the reputations of sellers in the retail market. If you're on Amazon, you're more likely to buy—and possibly pay more—without trepidation if you see sellers with positive marks from other buyers. The opposite is also true. If you see a seller with negative reviews, you're less likely to buy from them.

As a long-time wholesaler puts it, "Buyers are like elephants. They haven't got time to waste, and they remember *everything*."

Three Key Drivers of a Positive Seller Reputation

If you boil down the reasons why some sellers build the trust with buyers that leads to a positive reputation and others don't, you end up with three primary drivers.

80

The first driver relates to a seller's willingness to sell their vehicles. As we noted in the last chapter, the auction first-run sales efficiency rates of dealers suffer from their desire to get all the money they can from their wholesale vehicles. Bidders make their bids and sometimes believe they've purchased a vehicle, only to learn their final bid didn't meet the seller floor. This dynamic creates a condition some wholesalers refer to as "bidder fatigue."

A former wholesaler in the Midwest knows bidder fatigue all too well and seeks to avoid it as he sells his dealer group's vehicles at a biweekly auction. "We want to make sure all the cars run and sell," the manager says. "It doesn't take long to see the stress of the guys who have tromped in the snow or hot sun, and they're bidding on the car, and you don't sell it. They lose faith."

The upshot: The more willing you are to sell your car, the more likely you are, as a seller, to have buyers pay attention to your cars when they run at the auction.

A second driver of a positive seller reputation relates to transparency. The level of transparency required in the wholesale market depends on the value of a vehicle.

If you're taking a $5,000 vehicle to the auction as a seller, you get more bids from more potential buyers if you disclose what you know about the car. But you might still be able to sell the vehicle as-is, with little or no transparency about its condition. Why? Because there are some buyers who are specifically looking for vehicles that buyers from franchises and other stores wouldn't touch. The "as-is" buyer pool is smaller, but it's chock-full of individuals who know, going in with every potential wholesale purchase, that they can make the car work for them.

Here's how a long-time wholesaler puts it: "When a dealer or another seller sells everything as-is, you have a different buyer base. You have buyers who understand they're going to do crazy work to a car. They are sweat equity buyers. The sweat equity buyer knows it's got a slip in the transmission. The average buyer knows it's $2,700 to fix it. But this guy may even have one in the shop that he can swap out for $300."

For top-performing sellers, who are selling vehicles worth an average of $25,000 to $30,000, transparency is far more important. That's why companies like CarMax tout their ability to disclose vehicle conditions and histories to potential buyers before they ask them to bid on the vehicles.

By contrast, many dealers and managers prefer to disclose as little information as they can about a vehicle's condition. Sometimes they aren't aware of specific problems with a vehicle. Other times, they might be aware of the problem and prefer not to disclose it to avoid getting stuck with the vehicle or forced to sell it for far less than they think it's worth.

It's difficult to quantify how much this lack of transparency contributes to the less-than-optimal first-run sales efficiency rates dealers tend to see with their wholesale vehicles at auctions. Still, I think we can all agree that if a buyer has doubts about a seller's veracity related to a vehicle's condition, they are less likely to bid on and buy the seller's vehicles.

The third driver that leads to a positive seller reputation is the willingness to do the right thing when something is wrong with a car. I haven't done a formal study, but I understand it's rare for wholesale sellers to buy back a vehicle they just sold at auction with no questions asked if the buyer isn't happy. The lack of honesty or transparency about a vehicle's condition is a key reason auctions offer post-sale inspections, which can detect unknown problems and unwind a sale, and arbitration services to resolve concerns buyers raise about vehicles they just purchased from sellers at the auction.

Some dealers and wholesalers believe that dealers' first-run sales efficiency rates at Manheim auctions would be 10 percent higher if the post-sale inspection process was less rigorous and more friendly to sellers. That's why some wholesale sellers refer to post-sale inspections as "post-sale prevention."

But when I consider the frequency at which arbitration occurs at auctions—and the frustration and inefficiency it seems to create for buyers and sellers—I believe there's an opportunity for a better way. The better way would begin with more complete and thorough assessments of wholesale vehicle conditions *before* they get to the auction block. With a more complete and honest assessment of a vehicle's condition, sellers would have the opportunity to offer more holistic and transparent disclosures about their vehicles to buyers. They would also have a better idea of how much to pay for a vehicle and what they might expect in terms of its best wholesale price in a well-managed auction setting. They would have an incentive—and the means—to build a positive reputation.

In turn, buyers would be able to bid with more confidence. They would have fewer unknowns about each vehicle and fewer doubts that a vehicle is worth another bid. They would have a better idea of what they'd be willing to pay, since they know more about the car. Their list of preferred sellers would grow, based on positive purchase experiences. The better way might even bring a day when post-sale inspections would largely be unnecessary and, if buyers had legitimate concerns about the condition of a vehicle they purchased, the problems would likely be smaller and less significant than they are today.

I know. This sounds like pie-in-the-sky stuff.

But it isn't.

In fact, this is the way the team and I believe the wholesale market will function as new technologies and tools help usher in ways to fully capture a vehicle's condition, predict its best wholesale price, and greatly reduce—if not eliminate—the risks buyers and sellers face in the wholesale market today. You could say the better way will make buying and selling wholesale vehicles at auctions easier and friendlier for everyone involved—and it will forever and fully enable dealers to build a second barrel of profit-producing business in their used vehicle departments.

In subsequent chapters, we'll spend considerable time teasing out how technology and tools will help transform the wholesale market to doing business in a way the original wholesalers along Jerome Avenue and other places would have never thought possible.

But before we do that, let's examine how CarMax, Carvana, and other top-performing wholesale sellers measure their efforts to execute playbook principles and drive consistent profits when they sell wholesale vehicles at auctions. For the purposes of this discussion, I've distilled the complexity of these measurement efforts into what I've come to call the Rule of 200.

CHAPTER 14

THE RULE OF 200: MEASURING BEST WHOLESALE PRICE ACHIEVEMENT

A t the end of every auction sale as well as at the end of every month, top-performing wholesalers like CarMax or Carvana will assess two outcomes to measure how well their cars performed—and whether they made any money—at auction.

The first outcome assesses how many cars they were able to sell the first time they ran in the auction lanes—something that Manheim regards as first-run sales efficiency.

For the top-performing wholesalers, the goal is to sell 100 percent of the vehicles the first time, or at least the same day, they run in the lanes. As we've discussed in earlier chapters, when dealers sell all of their vehicles the first time they run, they are more likely to achieve best wholesale prices when the gavel falls and the vehicles sell. When vehicles don't sell, buyers suffer fatigue and they lose faith that a seller will let their bid stand and sell the vehicle. Meanwhile, buyers with a bit more patience will wait for the vehicle to run again, knowing the seller probably feels more urgency to sell the car at a lower price.

"Don't mistake buyers' brain levels for the way they dress," says a former wholesale buyer. "They are smart. They know if a car's run before, or it's run the past four weeks. As a buyer, that's the car I want. That normally means a bargain for me as a buyer."

The second outcome top-performing wholesalers assess is how well their vehicles performed against the market average for their vehicles. In the Manheim world, the wholesalers tell me they compare the sale price of each car against its Manheim Market Report (MMR) valuation and combine the cumulative scores to determine if the collective purchase prices or proceeds amount to 100 percent of MMR for all the vehicles.

Sellers understand if they achieve 100 percent of MMR combined for the vehicles they sell, they are meeting the market performance. If the cumulative average tops 100 percent of MMR, sellers know they are beating the market average.

Here's how the Rule of 200 works:

> *If you sell 100 percent of your vehicles the first time or on the first day they run at auctions, you receive a score of 100. If you only sell 50 percent of the vehicles, you'd score 50.*
>
> *If the cumulative sale of your vehicles achieves 100 percent of MMR, you'd receive a score of 100. If the cumulative sales of your vehicles only achieve 80 percent of MMR, you'd receive a score of 80.*
>
> *When dealers use the Rule of 200, the best score they could receive wouldn't necessarily be 200. If a*

dealer sold 100 percent of the vehicles, and achieved 103 percent of MMR, the dealer would achieve a score of 203—a stellar outcome by anyone's measure.

But the sad truth is that dealers and managers rarely come close to a score of 200.

We know that the average first-run sales efficiency rate for dealers runs roughly 50 percent, based on data from Cox Automotive's Manheim auctions we introduced in a previous chapter. We also know that only 55 percent of dealers consistently achieve 100 percent of MMR, while the remaining 45 percent falls short of this benchmark, sometimes by considerable margins.

If we applied the Rule of 200 to this data, we could say that roughly half of all dealers would score 160 on the scale of 200, and the rest would score even lower on the 200-point scale.

To me, this analysis suggests considerable room for improvement, and a significant opportunity for almost every dealer in America to build a double-barreled business in their used vehicle departments.

I especially appreciate the way the Rule of 200 would introduce a level of accountability and oversight into a dealer's wholesale operations that previously hasn't existed. The Rule of 200 offers a way to execute principles of the wholesale playbook and measure the outcomes.

If a dealer adopts the Rule of 200, some positive and significant things would start to happen. Some of the long-standing half-truths of wholesale would give way to a clearer view of the whole truth of a dealership's wholesaling activities.

Managers would know that their dealers were keeping score of the cars they took to auction. In fact, dealers might even start requiring all vehicles go to auction rather than wholesale buyers—if only to ensure a consistent method of managing and measuring these investments.

Dealers would readily know if "we got them all sold!" was a half- or whole truth of recent auction sales. If the first-run sales efficiency hits 100, there might be a conversation about the playbook principles that worked well and a resolution to remember their application the next time.

Managers and dealers would know if "we got more than MMR!" is true, or it isn't. They would know if their investments produced the average market return, or something more or less. If the cumulative sales of the vehicle fell short of total MMR, they could have a meaningful conversation about the cars that underperformed their best wholesale price expectations.

The Rule of 200 would move dealers and managers away from regarding wholesale vehicles as "trash" that needs a quick disposal. They would recognize the money-making potential inherent in their wholesale vehicle investments and actively achieve more profit-positive outcomes.

It is for all these reasons that the wholesale solution I've developed with the team is built with the principles of the wholesale playbook and the Rule of 200 in mind. The solution would offer dealers the means to execute wholesale playbook principles and build a second barrel of profit-producing business in the used vehicle department. The solution would effectively perform the same function as managers of index funds—ensuring that client investments meet or beat the market average on a regular basis.

I'll formally introduce the solution, known as Project Upside, and its vision in Chapter 16. In the meantime, I think it's useful to take a quick look at the history of index funds and how they helped tame inefficiencies in the financial markets that bear a striking resemblance to the inefficiencies that occur in the wholesale market every day.

CHAPTER 15

TWO SIMILAR MARKETS
AND THEIR LESSONS

F ifty years ago, if you invested in stocks or bonds, you likely had someone who took your money, picked the investments based on your desired risk and return, and managed your portfolio.

You paid this individual a commission, of course, to make decisions about whether your investments were good or bad. This individual also usually had discretion to move your money from one investment to another, based on their judgment about the investment's performance.

In good times, when your investment advisor or broker helped you make money, this individual was a hero. You didn't think about the cost of their expertise. In worse times, you might start hunting for an advisor or broker whose cost, reputation, or track record suggested you'd be better off financially.

This investment model bears a lot of similarities to the role managers in dealerships play as they handle a dealer's investments in used vehicles.

Often, the managers take a dealer's money and choose where to invest it. They decide which vehicles will become the dealer's investment. The managers also make decisions about whether the investments are good or bad. If it's a good investment, it'll likely be a retail unit. If it's a bad investment, it'll get wholesaled. In this way, the managers have discretion to move money from one investment to another, based on their judgment about the investment's performance.

In good times, when managers help their dealers make money, they are heroes. Dealers don't think about the cost of their investment-picking expertise. In worse times, dealers might start hunting for someone else whose cost, reputation, or track record suggests they'd be better off financially.

It's somewhat arresting to know that, in the 50 years since the advisor/broker model for investing was considered the norm, the financial markets and the way people invest has fundamentally changed. Today, index funds are largely the norm for individual investors. Investment advisors and brokers are no longer as popular or prevalent as they once were.

Meanwhile, the manager-based model for managing a dealer's investments in used vehicles hasn't changed much, if at all. Dealers still rely on individuals to make the best investment decisions on their behalf in a business that, as we've noted in earlier chapters, is beset by half-truth while the whole truth of wholesaling goes unknown.

As the team and I envisioned a new way forward for dealers in the wholesale market—one that would help them execute the principles of the wholesale playbook and consistently make money from their wholesale investments—the parallels to index fund investing kept coming up again and again. The role of this new solution, we reasoned, would be to provide the means for dealers to achieve index fund-like returns by providing greater insights to managers about wholesale values and how to sell the vehicles on behalf of dealers to achieve best wholesale prices—and investment returns—more consistently.

We found the history of index fund investing to be highly instructive and relevant for helping dealers and managers understand the advantages to taking a different approach to—and applying a different belief about—the prospect of making money from selling wholesale vehicles. In that spirit, here's a quick trip through the history of index fund investing and the lessons or parallels it offers to dealers and managers today.

A Different, Disruptive View of Investing Emerges

In 1974, a guy who was born in my hometown of Gary, IN, published an article that changed the world of financial investment forever.

The guy was the esteemed Nobel Prize-winning economist from the Massachusetts Institute of Technology, Paul Samuelson. His article, "Challenge to Judgement," appeared in the inaugural issue of the *Journal of Portfolio Management*.[2] The publication had been launched to provide a knowledge-building resource for the men and women who bought and sold investments on behalf of their clients.

---

2   Samuelson, Paul A. "Challenge to Judgment." *The Journal of Portfolio Management* 1, no. 1 (1974): 17–19. https://doi.org/10.3905/jpm.1974.408496.

At the time, intellectual heavy-hitters like Samuelson were taking newly available data to test theories on how financial markets worked and how they could create optimal financial outcomes for investors.

When Samuelson's article hit the streets, it caused a stir on Wall Street and beyond, including the oak-paneled and pipe smoke-filled studies of top academics. The article teases out Samuelson's belief that financial advisors and brokers who managed investments didn't consistently beat the market as often as they and others thought, particularly when you factored in the cost of their expertise, which he dubbed the "dead weight of commissions."

This line from the article had an especially sharp sting: "A respect for evidence compels me to incline toward the hypothesis that most portfolio decision makers should go out of business."

Samuelson asserted that while some advisors and brokers beat the market from time to time, their performance overtime was no better than if someone would put their money in a "passive" index fund of diverse investments. This fund wouldn't be "actively" managed, and it would feature lower fees, fewer overall transactions, and long-term returns that matched the overall performance of the market.

The article's "challenge" came in the following passage, wherein Samuelson issues a call for someone to set up an index fund that would provide "brute evidence" that "passive" funds could perform better than "active" funds with highly paid managers: "That, at the least, some large foundation set up an in-house portfolio that tracks the S&P 500 Index—if only for the purpose of setting up a naive model against which their in-house gunslingers can measure their prowess."

Some readers may know the rest of this story.

Samuelson's challenge provided inspiration to a guy from Bryn Mawr, PA: John "Jack" Bogle. He had been batting around the idea of an index-type fund since he wrote his senior thesis at Princeton University in the early 1950s. When he read Samuelson's article, he went to work.

"(Samuelson) laid down an express challenge for somebody, somewhere to start an index fund," Bogle wrote in a 2011 piece for the *Wall Street Journal*. "Presented with that challenge, I couldn't stand back any longer."[3]

In 1975, Bogle created the Vanguard Group, which launched the first index fund. He outlines the early effort in the *WSJ* piece:

"While all of our peers had the opportunity to create the first index fund, Vanguard alone had the motivation . . . For our goal was to offer well-diversified funds at minimal costs, focused on the long term. It was a marriage, as it were, made in heaven, strongly supported by the unequivocal data I assembled on fund performance and fund costs over the previous three decades. It was the opportunity of a lifetime: to at once prove that indexing could work in practice as well as in theory, and work effectively, and to mark this upstart of a firm as a pioneer in a new wave of industry development. With Dr. Samuelson's inspiration, and with luck and hard work, the idea that had begun to germinate in my mind in my Princeton thesis would finally become a reality."

Today, the Vanguard Group is literally a household name. The company manages $6.2 trillion in assets and ranks as the largest

---

3   Bogle, John C. "How the Index Fund Was Born." *Wall Street Journal*. Dow Jones & Company, September 3, 2011. https://www.wsj.com/articles/SB10001424053111904583204576544681577401622.

mutual fund provider in the world, according to the company's website. I've got money invested in Vanguard funds, and I suspect many readers do, too. They are often considered the gold standard by which index fund investing is measured.

Parallels to Improving Wholesale Profit Performance

With the emergence of data science and technology that can help predict best wholesale prices for vehicles, I began to shape a wholesale solution that would help evolve the wholesale market in ways that index funds reshaped the business of individual investing. Broadly speaking, there are four ways that index funds changed investing for the better:

1. **A broader mix of investment types and returns.** The best financial advisors and brokers have their favorite types of investments, and they spend at least part of their time investigating where the next great investment might come from. They also work their portfolios from the individual investment on up, that is, they put a greater emphasis on making the winners work while moving away from, or out of entirely, their poor-performing investments. The same dynamics are true with dealership managers. They're often cherry-picking the cars for retail and wholesale exits, and sometimes combining winners from both to make the financial statement show a favorable outcome.

Losing cars, like losing investments, get left behind in the quest to get the next big money-maker. An index fund-like approach to buying and selling wholesale vehicles would bring more balance to a dealer's entire portfolio of wholesale vehicle investments and provide a means to measure the totality of their outcomes as the vehicles are sold in the wholesale market.

2. **Less emphasis on expertise**. Samuelson used the term "flair" to describe the acumen of individual investors, whose reputations for picking investments often lagged their actual performance at meeting or beating the market average over the long term. It's a similar situation in dealerships. Good used vehicle and wholesale managers can correctly pick winning and losing vehicles from time to time, but the losses or even small gains that show up on the financials suggest they, too, aren't consistently achieving the market average returns on wholesale investments.

3. **A focus on achieving the market average**. Samuelson's gripe about investment managers is that their occasional, celebrated wins masked the reality of their suboptimal performance over the long term. Dealers and managers also tend to focus on the latest and greatest outcome from the sale of a wholesale vehicle (e.g., "we got more than MMR!"). Today, dealers and managers have the opportunity to broaden their focus to the totality of their wholesale performance and use wholesale playbook principles and

the Rule of 200 to work toward meeting—or beating—the market average for their wholesale vehicle sales.

4. **Greater access to meaningful investment returns**. One of the reasons I'm drawn to intellects like Samuelson is that, at a fundamental level, he cared about what's right for the common good. He believed that financial markets should work for the benefit of many, not just a few. He worried that highly paid investment managers made more for themselves than their clients. He viewed the index fund as a means for more people to gain access to—and gain greater benefit from—participation in the financial markets. I believe the same scenario is true today for dealers. An index fund-styled approach to managing wholesale investments offers a way for dealers to enjoy the returns that top-performing wholesalers like CarMax and Carvana consistently achieve. In turn, the wholesale market itself will work better for all participants and stakeholders.

That's the history and relevance of a new solution that I believe can help dealers build a profitable, second barrel of business in their used vehicle departments.

Let's take a closer look.

CHAPTER 16

PROJECT UPSIDE VISION: ELIMINATE RISK, PROVIDE GUARANTEED PROFITS FOR DEALERS

When you consider the whole truth of wholesaling vehicles for dealers, it represents a long history of suboptimal outcomes.

You've got dealers and managers selling cars directly to wholesalers. The wholesalers buy the cars and resell them for a profit. In this way, they may provide a convenient way for dealers to get rid of wholesale units. But, in exchange for the convenience, wholesalers are extracting value from a dealer's wholesale operations. The greater the value they extract from dealers, the more money the wholesalers and others make when the vehicles sell in the wholesale market.

Dealers and managers also achieve suboptimal outcomes at auctions, including the digital auctions that have come on the scene in recent years with a promise of greater wholesaling ease, lower fees, and more transparency. As I've tried to lay out in previous chapters, the suboptimal performance for dealers at auctions seems due to a combination of a lack of appreciation for or interest in the proper execution of wholesale playbook principles, as well as the long-held belief that losses or small profits are to be expected when you take a car to auction.

The suboptimal outcomes dealers traditionally realize from selling wholesale vehicles also owe to two current, long-standing realities of the wholesale market.

1. **Regardless of how dealers and managers dispose of their wholesale vehicles, they usually bear all the risk.** The risk, of course, is that the dealer won't recover the money they paid to acquire the vehicle. Dealers and managers often try to hedge this risk by setting floors or minimum bid requirements on auction vehicles that ensure they won't lose money—a practice that typically makes it even more difficult for them to get all the money—or best wholesale prices—when the vehicles eventually sell.

2. **None of the ways that dealers wholesale vehicles today provides a guaranteed profit on every vehicle they wholesale.** Dealers may get a guaranteed offer for a vehicle, but such offers aren't intended to help dealers make money off the car. The offers are meant to ensure the individual or company that offers the guarantee makes money when they resell the vehicle.

Against this backdrop, the team and I asked what seemed like a far-fetched question: Could we find a way to guarantee that dealers would make money every time they wholesale a vehicle and eliminate the risk dealers face today with every wholesale investment?

To answer the question, we began to sketch out a solution that would draw from the lessons top-performing wholesalers offer through their consistently solid execution of wholesale play-book principles. We also drew from the Rule of 200 and the index investing principles that economist Paul Samuelson imagined and that Vanguard's Jack Bogle put into practice years ago. Next, we tasked data scientists and developers at Cox Automotive and vAuto to figure out if it would be possible to predict a vehicle's best wholesale price with some degree of accuracy and consistency and—if the sale of auction vehicles were properly managed on a dealer's behalf—how much of a profit we might be able to guarantee dealers on every car.

This is how the wholesale industry's first managed disposition service—that will guarantee a profit on every car and eliminate risk or loss for dealers—was born. The team and I have given the solution a working name: Project Upside.

Why Upside? The name is intended to reflect the profit-positive outcomes all of us expect will flow to dealers' financial bottom lines as we introduce the solution. The Upside name also reflects the reality that the new solution will deliver more financial upside for dealers than their present mode of wholesaling vehicles—through wholesalers, going it alone at auction, or experimenting with fledgling start-up digital auctions—can deliver.

A Money-Making, Risk-Reducing Model

Perhaps the most challenging question I encountered was determining how much minimum profit the service could guarantee a dealer for every wholesale vehicle it sells for a best wholesale price on a dealer's behalf. The amount would, of course, need to account for the risk Project Upside would incur when a vehicle it sells on a dealer's behalf does not achieve its predicted best wholesale price. Project Upside must then make good on its promise to pay the dealer a minimum guaranteed profit.

I turned to data science to help. The Project Upside team and I soon understood that, with a proper baseline wholesale value for a vehicle and well-executed wholesale playbook principles, suboptimal vehicle sales and consequential losses must be expected. The

PROJECT UPSIDE'S GUARANTEED PROFIT MODEL

Here's a quick look at how Project Upside will guarantee a minimum profit and eliminate risk for dealers as it sells wholesale vehicles on their behalf.

When a dealer uses Project Upside to obtain a baseline wholesale value for a vehicle and chooses to let the solution sell the vehicle on his/her behalf, the dealer would be guaranteed a minimum profit of $300, plus 90 percent of any upside when the vehicle sells.

For example, if Project Upside says the vehicle is worth $15,000, the dealer would get at least $15,300 for the vehicle when it sells (the $15,000 value, plus the minimum guaranteed profit of $300). In addition, if the vehicle sells for more than $15,300, Project Upside would give 90 percent of the upside back to the dealer. For example, if the $15,000 vehicle sold for $16,000 at the auction, the dealer would receive an additional $630, which represents the dealer's share of the $700 upside.

In this scenario, the total profit for the dealer would be $965, an amount that arrives with no risk. Meanwhile, Project Upside would retain $70 for managing the vehicle's sale at the auction on behalf of the dealer.

law of averages dictates that some cars will sell below their best wholesale prices. The key, of course, will be Project Upside's ability to use the law of averages to its advantage, much the way index funds do. Project Upside will need to carefully curate and manage the sale of every car on behalf of a dealer to the best of our ability if we expect to achieve best wholesale prices more times than not.

The team and I landed on an initial "launch" model that we think represents a win-win for dealers and the solution. The working model sets the following baselines, which are subject to change as Project Upside takes flight, to guarantee a profit and minimize risk for dealers: When dealers assign a vehicle to Project Upside using the system's baseline wholesale value, Project Upside will guarantee a minimum $300 in profit. When the vehicle sells, Project Upside will give dealers 90 percent of any upside the vehicle receives when it sells. The upside would be calculated by subtracting Project Upside's baseline wholesale value and the $300 minimum guaranteed profit from the vehicle's sale price in the wholesale market (see sidebar, previous page, for an example).

The Project Upside model asks two up-front commitments from dealers to participate—a commitment to assigning 100 percent of their wholesale-destined trade-ins to Project Upside and paying a nominal monthly subscription fee that will replace traditional auction seller fees. This cost of entry is necessary to ensure Project Upside doesn't suffer from adverse selection. For the Project Upside system to work for a dealer's money-making benefit over the long term, the system needs the good, bad, and ugly vehicles a dealer's typical mix of wholesale vehicles represents. Just like index funds, Project Upside functions best from a diverse mix of investments.

Project Upside's money-making model likely raises an immediate concern for many dealers and managers. They might say, "Sure, you'll give me a guaranteed profit of $300, but it's based on a low-ball number for the car."

It's a valid concern or objection. It's often based on experience, where some wholesalers might offer a guaranteed value for a vehicle that is, in fact, a lowball number. The wholesalers who offer the guarantee fully intend to sell the vehicle for more than the guaranteed amount. Their end game is to retain the lion's share, if not all, of the profit that they expect to make when the vehicle sells in the wholesale market.

But Project Upside is different. A Project Upside valuation for a vehicle isn't a lowball number—it's just a starting point. It's a baseline wholesale value.

On top of that, Project Upside intends to give the lion's share of the upside profit—90 percent—when the vehicle sells back to the dealer. In my view, this approach is far more dealer-favorable and -friendly than any "guarantees" they might receive from other companies. Project Upside's approach is exactly the opposite of other wholesalers—rather than extract value, the solution delivers it to the dealer.

I would 100 percent agree that Project Upside's baseline wholesale valuation *would* be a lowball number if it intended to keep the lion's share of profit from a wholesale vehicle for itself. That's simply not the case given Project Upside's plans to share 90 percent of the upside profit, in addition to a minimum $300 in guaranteed profit for each vehicle.

Some readers might also be asking why Project Upside would

want to share profits when they sell wholesale vehicles on behalf of dealers through Project Upside rather than keep it themselves.

I'm confident when I say that I believe it's the right thing to do. After all, the investment in the vehicle represents the dealer's money. The dealer and his/her team in the dealership took the time and effort to acquire the vehicle from the customer. We believe there should be some reward for dealers who opt to use Project Upside and entrust their investment—and the risk it represents—to the service. We view the sharing of profits derived from achieving best wholesale prices for a dealer's vehicles as part of our collective mission to transform the way the world buys and sells vehicles for the better. We don't want to be in the business of extracting value from dealers: We want to provide more value and place it where it rightfully belongs.

My goal for this chapter is to help dealers understand the foundational vision for Project Upside and how it seeks to upend the current status quo of the wholesale market by offering guaranteed profit and no risk for their wholesale vehicles. Now, let's turn our attention to how Project Upside would manage the vehicles and their auction sales to generate best wholesale prices that enable its profit-generating and -sharing model.

CHAPTER 17

HOW PROJECT UPSIDE ACHIEVES BEST WHOLESALE PRICES

There's an old saying in the car business that the best way to get into a vehicle is to know how you'll get out of it.

The saying is a foundational principle of retail-focused acquisition and pricing strategies that dealers have deployed in their used vehicle department for much of the past 15 years. It's also a foundation for how Project Upside will use best practices of the wholesale playbook to manage the sale of a dealer's wholesale vehicles and achieve best wholesale prices that enable it to guarantee profits and eliminate risk for its dealer clients.

In recent years, Cox Automotive has added data science capabilities to its creed. It's spent time trying to understand how and where it can improve its auction settings—and the rules that govern the sale of wholesale vehicles—to bring greater benefit to buyers and sellers. It's studied what the best wholesalers—entities like Carvana and Vroom—do with their vehicles to consistently achieve the Rule of 200 and realize best wholesale prices for their vehicles.

Cox Automotive has worked to understand the linkage between properly executed principles of the wholesale playbook and the proceeds and profits that often follow. It's taken time to understand how buyers prefer to purchase wholesale vehicles and how a higher degree of transparency about a vehicle's condition might be a game-changer. It's also kept an eye on companies that have entered the wholesale marketplace, seeking to provide greater convenience and efficiency for dealers who need to wholesale vehicles and buyers who want to purchase them.

Through all this work, the Project Upside team has developed a system that enables the service to project a vehicle's best wholesale price; offer an Actual Cash Value (ACV) or baseline wholesale valuation for a dealer's vehicle; and then manage the sale of the vehicle to achieve its best wholesale price, all while guaranteeing profits and eliminating risk for dealers.

A Clear View of a Vehicle's Condition

If you study the economic theories about auctions and how they work, there's been a great deal of brainpower devoted to understanding the behaviors of buyers and sellers and how they shape the outcomes or purchase prices of goods or services that go up for sale. If you're curious about an aspect of how and why auctions work, chances are you'll find an academic paper on the topic.

In 2020, two prominent economists from Stanford University won the Nobel Prize for Economics for work that examined how a bidder's perception of risk results in less-aggressive bidding (see sidebar, this page).

I'd venture that most dealers and managers, especially those who've spent any significant time buying and selling vehicles at auctions, don't need an academic study to prove what they've learned from experience about bidders and perceived risks. If they're buying a car, for example, they know that if they have any significant questions about a vehicle's condition, they're likely to bid and pay less than if they were more certain that a vehicle's condition wouldn't pose any problems.

It's fascinating, if not ironic, that while dealers and managers are acutely sensitive to risk when they're buying cars, they don't care as much about it when they're selling a vehicle to someone else. As buyers, dealers and managers pay super close attention to vehicle condition reports and histories as they purchase vehicles.

HOW TRANSPARENCY DRIVES BIDDING

Stanford University economists Robert Wilson and Paul Milgrom won the Nobel Prize for Economics in October 2020 for their work in auction theory.

Part of the work that earned the pair the Nobel Prize focused on how a "winner's curse" can cause auction bidders to be afraid of over-paying, which results in less aggressive bids and less than optimal returns for sellers. The economists suggested a solution for the problem—sellers should provide more information about the item being sold to minimize a bidder's perception of risk.

An Associated Press article summarized it this way: *"A solution, according to the research by Wilson and Milgram, is for the seller to provide as much information as possible before the bidding begins, perhaps providing an independent appraisal of the item being sold. Solving the problem doesn't just help the seller get a better price; it helps make sure the item being auctioned goes to the bidder likely to make the most efficient use of it."* [1]

(continued)

As sellers, they are far less committed to clarity and transparency about a vehicle's condition.

On one hand, you can understand this duality. If a dealer or manager knows a vehicle they've acquired from a customer is headed to wholesale right away and they expect to lose or break even on the car when it sells,

Such principles drive the way Project Upside will account for and disclose the condition of every wholesale vehicle it sells. Project Upside's higher level of vehicle condition transparency will be a win-win, for the dealers who use the system and the buyers who purchase their wholesale vehicles.

what's the incentive to provide a greater level of transparency? What's the point of an appraiser or technician spending any more time than they've already invested on the vehicle, especially if they uncover a problem that makes the vehicle unlikely to sell at all?

The answers to these questions rest in the data science. Data from Cox Automotive's Manheim auctions, for example, shows that when vehicles underperform at auction, and achieve less than the Manheim Market Report (MMR) or don't sell, a chief culprit relates to unknowns about the vehicle's condition.

It is for this reason that, if a dealer wants to use Project Upside to help build a second barrel of profit-producing business in their used vehicle departments, the dealer will need to ensure a higher level of clarity and transparency about the condition of vehicles they ask Project Upside to sell on their behalf at auctions. The fact

1   Keyton, David, Frank Jordans, and Paul Wiseman. "2 Stanford Economists Win Nobel Prize for Improving Auctions." AP NEWS. Associated Press, October 12, 2020. https://apnews.com/article/stockholm-ap-top-news-international-news-ca-state-wire-virus-outbreak-3e2cbe8c2ee8c8bb83783120c16de9e6.

is, Project Upside won't be able to generate an accurate or reliable baseline value for the vehicle, guarantee a minimum profit to the dealer, or expect a best wholesale price for the vehicle when it sells if it can't give buyers the whole truth about the car.

Of course, Project Upside can help dealers and managers capture more detail and truth about a vehicle's condition if they don't want to do it themselves. Project Upside will offer concierge-like experience, where representatives can, for a nominal fee, assess the vehicle's condition and get the necessary photos and other information compiled to list the vehicle in online and physical auctions.

But I believe there's an even better upside for dealers if, rather than outsource the assessment and documentation of a vehicle's condition, they make a concerted effort to transform their appraisal process so at least some of the essential descriptive work about a vehicle's condition gets handled by the customer, irrespective of whether the vehicle will be a retail or a wholesale unit. (The next chapter offers a detailed look at how a reimagined appraisal process might work with Project Upside in the picture.)

How Project Upside Sells the Vehicles

Once Project Upside knows enough about the vehicle to generate a real and relevant wholesale value, and a dealer or manager has decided to use the system to manage the vehicle's sale in the wholesale market, it will begin the effort to achieve the best wholesale prices for the vehicles.

The vehicles themselves wouldn't necessarily need to leave the dealer's lot with Project Upside. It will use a combination of online and physical auctions. The specific auction setting will depend on the vehicle, geography, and what data science suggests would be the most optimal place, time, and method to match the vehicle to buyers who are most likely to be the best buyers.

When Project Upside places a car to the wholesale auction setting, it will do four things that are essential to achieve a best wholesale price for every vehicle:

1. **Ensure a curated critical quantity of vehicles that buyers will want to purchase**. Project Upside has a size advantage over other players in the wholesale market. Partnering with Manheim marketplaces, Project Upside will benefit from the largest wholesale marketplaces, where there are more buyers and more available cars, than anywhere else in the world. Like other top-performing wholesalers who thrive in these marketplaces, Project Upside will ensure that the vehicles it represents will run when, where, and how they make the most sense. There won't be what some describe as a "spaghetti eyes" marketplace with no rhyme or reason why some vehicles run together. Project Upside sales will be carefully curated to ensure vehicles with similar characteristics and traits (SUVs, pick-ups, luxury sedans, etc.) are combined to appeal to a maximum number of highly motivated buyers.

2. **Provide the transparency highly motivated buyers require**. As I noted earlier in this chapter, a clear view of a vehicle's true

condition, warts and all, is essential to generate best wholesale prices. The goal for Project Upside-managed vehicle sales is the same as other top-performing wholesalers—provide cars and assessments of their conditions that buyers will believe and trust. As Project Upside becomes known for clarity and transparency about a vehicle's condition, buyers will have greater confidence about a vehicle and less risk-related uncertainty. Over time, I believe more buyers and vehicles will come to its managed marketplaces, and best wholesale prices will follow.

3. **Aim to sell every vehicle**. There's nothing worse for buyers—or the first-run sales efficiency rates of sellers—than setting minimum reserves, or floors, on wholesale vehicles that aren't realistic or representative of the vehicle's actual value. By contrast, Project Upside will effectively start vehicles at a percentage of MMR value that data science suggests will spur buyers to bid—much like Vroom did when it opened bidding with floors at roughly 50 percent of the MMR value of each vehicle. Project Upside takes on the risk if, in a particular moment with a specific vehicle, the best wholesale price falls below expectations. If that happens, the dealer doesn't bear any risk. He/she still receives at least a minimum guaranteed profit of $300 for the vehicle, while Project Upside eats the loss. Despite this risk, the Project Upside team and I believe that effective execution of wholesale playbook principles, which includes buyers understanding that the Project Upside intends to sell

every vehicle, will result in vehicles achieving their optimal best wholesale prices rather than falling short. In turn, as buyers know they won't suffer bidder fatigue in Project Upside-curated sales, they'll bid on and buy its vehicles.

4. **Eliminate risk for buyers**. In addition to eliminating risk for the dealers who use Project Upside to manage the sale of their wholesale vehicles, the service will also work to eliminate risk for buyers. This risk-elimination effort begins with greater transparency about a vehicle's condition and extends to the way Project Upside will handle any buyer concerns about the vehicle they just purchased. Like other top-performing wholesalers who take back cars when buyers raise significant concerns that the vehicle wasn't accurately represented in the auction sale, Project Upside will do right for buyers who purchase vehicles from its managed marketplaces. Meanwhile, the dealers Project Upside represents will remain whole. They won't be on the hook when buyers balk. They're still guaranteed the $300 minimum in profit for the vehicle, and they may earn even more when Project Upside works to resell the vehicle and achieve its best wholesale price.

A Focus on the Long-Term

To be sure, Project Upside's business model doesn't represent a can't-lose proposition. The fact is, Project Upside will lose on cars all the time. The sale prices of the wholesale vehicles will sometimes fall short of the amount Project Upside has guaranteed the dealer for the vehicle and the initial $300 profit. There will also be times when Project Upside achieves a best wholesale price for a vehicle and, for whatever reason, the buyer wants out. Such are the circumstances and costs that Project Upside carries as it takes on the risk that previously fell to dealers and other sellers of wholesale vehicles.

But Project Upside will also break even on some vehicles, and it'll win on some vehicles. In this way, the solution is banking on the same law of win-lose-and-draw averages over the long haul that economist Paul Samuelson and Vanguard founder Jack Bogle proved can consistently produce market returns.

I believe that if we do things right, the losses Project Upside incurs will decline over time, both in frequency and in dollars. Such is the nature of bringing a better, more efficient and transparent way of doing business to a marketplace that has lacked efficiency and transparency for decades.

In some ways, Project Upside reflects my belief that any solution's success in the car business is inextricably tied to the wholesale and retail clients it serves. Dealers who use Project Upside to wholesale vehicles will benefit from consistently achieving profits for their wholesale vehicles while freeing themselves from any downside risk. Wholesale buyers, meanwhile, will benefit from a more efficient marketplace where they have more confidence in the vehicles they purchase and less risk of buying vehicles that turn out to be less than what they expected.

I have no doubt that Project Upside will benefit from its efforts to make the wholesale market more efficient and a better place to do business for buyers and sellers.

Ultimately, the key to Project Upside's success will largely rest on whether its value proposition for dealers—a guarantee of profit and zero risk—will be enough to overcome the deeply rooted culture of half-truths that are often baked into the way dealers and managers appraise and value the vehicles they acquire from customers and choose to wholesale.

Now, let's have a look at how a dealer's appraisal process might look when they use Project Upside to build a second barrel of profit-producing business in their used vehicle departments.

CHAPTER 18

AN ACTIVE METHOD TO ACHIEVE DOUBLE-BARRELED APPRAISALS

I n today's used vehicle marketplace, the process dealers use to appraise vehicles is more important than it's ever been.

Dealers, managers, and sales associates know that many, if not most, customers who bring in a vehicle to sell or trade have done their research online. They have a number in mind that they should get for the vehicle. Some may even have guaranteed purchase prices from entities like Kelley Blue Book Instant Cash Offer that they'll have in hand or on a mobile phone when they engage a dealer.

If a dealer hopes to acquire the customer's car, the offer their appraisers, managers, and sales associates make for a vehicle must at least come close to meeting customer expectations. If a customer isn't satisfied with the offer, they'll take the car somewhere else in search of the money they believe the vehicle is worth.

At the same time, the appraisal process itself is undergoing reinvention, much of which has been driven by the COVID-19 pandemic and the rise of retailers like Carvana and Vroom, who are willing to appraise and purchase vehicles from customers at their homes. More traditional dealers in many markets have begun adopting new processes and tools to complete "sight unseen" appraisals so they can be more competitive and compelling options for customers looking to sell or trade in their vehicle without coming to a physical dealership.

On top of all this, dealers need the cars their customers want to sell or trade. As we've noted earlier in the book, wholesale supplies are lean and low, and wholesale prices have been sky-high for much of 2021—conditions that will likely be with us for some time. Dealers and managers know that if they can acquire a vehicle from a customer, they'll be able to bring the vehicle into their inventories at a Cost to Market percentage that's far more favorable for front-end gross profit potential than anything they can acquire from an auction or the broader wholesale market.

These conditions have led more dealers and managers to focus more attention, energy, and time on fine-tuning their appraisal processes. Generally speaking, they are paying more attention to Look to Book and Cost to Market percentages for individual appraisers to determine if/when they may be missing cars they should acquire.

But despite the oversight and efforts to standardize the way appraisers evaluate vehicles and do a good job, it's not unusual for the actual process of appraising vehicles to fall short. These shortcomings manifest irrespective of whether an appraiser or manager knows the vehicle will be a retail or wholesale unit from the moment they see it.

The first shortcoming relates to the appraisal process. In today's environment, if appraisers are appraising vehicles without physically examining them with a customer (the proverbial "arm-chair" or "desk chair" appraisal method), chances are better than good the offer and process will fall short of many customers' expectations. Further, the disinterest in the car's physical condition may result in a big miss on the part of the appraiser's estimate of the vehicle's baseline wholesale value, or the value a manager might use to conduct a retail-back assessment if the vehicle will become a retail vehicle.

A second shortcoming relates to the accuracy and quality of the appraiser's assessment of the mechanical and physical condition of the vehicle when they do physically examine a vehicle. For mechanical assessments, it's imperative that the appraiser drives the car. If the drive doesn't happen, there's no basis for the mechanical assessment. In addition, it's not uncommon for dealers to use the standard reconditioning estimate. If we look at inventory data from dealers using vAuto, we see that the standard appraiser reconditioning estimates average $1,000 for late-model vehicles and about $400 for older vehicles.

The practice of using standard reconditioning estimates often has unintended and unnoticed consequences. For one thing, it creates a temptation to rush through the physical examination of the vehicle. You don't need to listen, look, and sniff close to the interior, exterior, and mechanical condition of the vehicle if you know there's a $1,000 backstop to catch what you might miss.

In addition, if the actual reconditioning costs end up being much lower than the estimate, the effective credit to the vehicle's actual cost can make an appraiser's or manager's decision for a wholesale or retail exit land off the mark. For example, if a vehicle's $1,000 reconditioning cost estimate spurs a manager to wholesale the vehicle and the actual cost turns out to be significantly less, the wholesale exit might have been the wrong decision. On the flip side, if the $1,000 estimate is used for a retail-back assessment and the actual cost should be $500, the vehicle's retail price and gross profit margin won't be accurate.

A third shortcoming links to what is known as the "silent walkaround," wherein the appraiser, often with a customer, walks the vehicle without engaging the customer. We did plenty of silent walkarounds at my dealership back in the day. It was, in fact, regarded as a best practice at the time. Today, however, the silent walkaround has the opposite effect with customers. If the appraiser isn't engaging the customer in this phase of the appraisal, it creates mystery and suspicion for the customer. They simply don't like not knowing what's going on. The result of this shortcoming is that the customer will probably push back on whatever offer your appraiser decides to make.

How Project Upside Solves Appraisal Shortcomings

Project Upside seeks to put an end to these appraisal process shortcomings. The end goal is to help dealers build a second barrel of profitable wholesale business while optimizing their retail barrel of business. The foundation for how Upside will help dealers achieve these positive double-barreled outcomes is what is currently known as an "active appraisal" process.

Let's have a look at how active appraisals work and three very important things they help dealers accomplish.

1. **Active appraisals ensure a more customer-focused and -friendly process.** Active appraisals occur *with* customers, whether they are at the dealership or using online tools like Kelley Blue Book Instant Cash Offer to get a value for their vehicle. If the customer and car is at your store, the appraiser and the customer would walk the vehicle together. If they are somewhere else, your appraiser and the customer would have a two-way exchange to virtually appraise the car, using information the customer provides.

2. In a dealership setting, the active appraisal process would have the appraiser and customer examining the car together. The appraiser would note any damage or dings that might affect a vehicle's value. There would be a conversation, wherein the appraiser might ask the customer what he/she does or doesn't like about the vehicle and the story behind any obvious issues with the interior and exterior of the car. The appraiser would have a camera, taking pictures of the good and not-so-good aspects of the vehicle.

3. The active appraisal process would also include an assessment of the mechanical condition of the vehicle. The appraiser would test-drive the car to assess the condition of its engine, suspension, and transmission. The appraiser might also use a technology-enabled tool that allows a quick read on the health of the vehicle's electrical and

mechanical components. The appraiser would review his/
her assessment with the customer to complete the appraisal
in the Upside system.

4. **Project Upside's active appraisal process brings to
   dealers a fuller, more accurate assessment of the vehicle's
   actual condition**. The process ensures that Project Upside
   knows enough about the car, from the good to the bad, to
   generate a baseline wholesale value, guarantee a profit, and
   eliminate all the risk if the dealer chooses to wholesale the
   vehicle. In addition, if a vehicle is intended to be a retail
   unit, the active appraisal process ensures a better-informed,
   more accurate basis of the vehicle's current condition to
   determine a reconditioning estimate.

5. **Project Upside's active appraisal process ensures dealers and
   managers will be in a much better position to determine
   whether the vehicle should be a wholesale or a retail unit**.
   For example, if the system generates a baseline wholesale
   value for a vehicle of $15,000, the dealer or manager would
   know that they could assign the vehicle to Project Upside
   for $15,000 and receive a minimum of $300 in guaranteed
   profit, plus 90 percent of the upside if it sells for more than
   $15,300. If the dealer or manager plans to retail the vehicle,
   they would at least have a far more accurate reconditioning
   estimate to plug into their retail back assessment to determine
   the vehicle's front-end gross profit margin and retail asking
   price (see sidebar, next page).

"RETAIL-OUT" MATH AND PROJECT UPSIDE

It's important for dealers and managers to recognize that the way they determine their "retail-out" strategy for a vehicle doesn't change with Project Upside and the baseline wholesale value it generates.

In fact, the system's baseline wholesale value is essentially irrelevant when you know you've got a retail car and you're trying to determine how much to offer or pay the customer for the vehicle. In these instances, you would still use prevailing retail asking prices, and subtract reconditioning and other costs you assign to retail cars and your minimum profit, to find the amount to offer or pay the customer.

Perhaps the biggest benefit Project Upside's active appraisal process provides dealers and managers with retail vehicles is the more accurate assessment of a vehicle's condition and the reconditioning costs required to retail it.

Ultimately, as dealers and managers know, you can pay more than a baseline wholesale value for a vehicle if you intend to retail it. The amount you pay should always be determined from understanding where you'll need to price the vehicle and the costs associated with making it a retail unit.

Some readers might be asking, "Wait a second, are you saying that, if I'm using Project Upside, I should be using its baseline wholesale value to make offers to customers? And, if that's the case, what if the customer in your example doesn't accept $15,000 as the value for the vehicle? I won't be able to make deals with that number."

The answer to the first question is "yes," IF you determine the customer's vehicle will be sold right away as a wholesale unit through Project Upside. That's because the system operates from the baseline wholesale value it generates. Project Upside uses the baseline wholesale value to guarantee a minimum profit and predict the vehicle's best wholesale price when it sells the vehicle.

The answer to the second question is that you can always over-allow to acquire the vehicle, provided you account for the over-allowance differently than you probably have in the past.

But I would submit that if your appraisers follow an active appraisal process with the customer, and they have both assessed and talked about the various aspects of the condition that affect the vehicle's value, the customer is more likely to consider Project Upside's baseline wholesale value as a reasonable offer, regardless of the valuation estimate or figure they might have found for themselves online.

Why? Because the two-way appraisal process is honest, open, and transparent. It's not a subjective conversation about what the vehicle's worth. It's not a debate over a trade-in offer that resulted from an appraisal that occurred while the customer was waiting inside the dealership and was oblivious to the appraiser's assessment. It's a valuation based on objective facts about the car's condition that the appraiser and customer discussed together. The customer would understand that the active appraisal is a better-informed evaluation of the vehicle than the one he/she might have completed online. In fact, dealers who use Kelley Blue Book Instant Cash Offer in conjunction with an active appraisal process report the same outcomes—customers are less likely to push back because they trust and understand the appraisal process.

A moment ago, I mentioned the need for dealers using Project Upside to handle the costs of over-allowances differently. I know it's a touchy subject that might meet some resistance.

That's exactly why I've devoted the next chapter to detailing how dealers can account for the costs of trade-in over-allowances in a new way—one that will help, rather than hurt, their ability to improve profitability in their retail and wholesale barrels of used vehicle business.

CHAPTER 19

HOW ACTUAL CASH VALUE "BUMPS" IMPERIL YOUR DOUBLE-BARRELED OPPORTUNITY

One of the long-standing half-truths in the used vehicle business relates to the Actual Cash Value (ACV) dealers and managers assign to used vehicles.

In fact, one could go a step further and state that, in many cases, the ACV on a used vehicle is worse than a half-truth. It's a lie. The ACV does not reflect what a dealer or manager could get for the vehicle if they sold it right now. Rather, the ACV reflects the value a dealer or manager *prefers* to assign to the vehicle, often based on the circumstances of a related new or used vehicle deal. Instead of the Actual Cash Value, this measure of a vehicle's value becomes what might be called the Adjusted Cash Value.

We all know why ACVs become less than truthful: Dealers and managers bump ACVs to cover the cost of over-allowances on customer trades. It's a practice many believe is essential to making deals and keeping customers happy. After all, there's often a lot of daylight between an appraiser's valuation of a vehicle and the amount a customer expects to receive if they sell or trade in their vehicle. I would also submit that the degree of daylight, particularly in areas where companies like Carvana and Vroom are proactively acquiring vehicles directly from customers, is often bigger today than it has been in the past.

But as dealers consider the opportunity to use Project Upside to build a double-barreled business in their used vehicle departments, it's important that everyone understands why the long-standing practices of bumping the ACVs to cover the cost of a trade-in over-allowance will make it difficult, if not impossible, to generate consistent and sizable profits from selling the vehicles in the wholesale market, and it will sub-optimize outcomes for retail vehicles.

Let me be clear: I am *not* suggesting that dealers and managers cannot over-allow for trade-ins when they use Project Upside. I know as well as anyone else how critical this practice can be to making new and used car deals. In the next chapter, I'll suggest better, more truthful ways to handle the cost of over-allowances that ensures the ACV on a vehicle remains true to the vehicle's actual wholesale value.

Here, I want to focus on what might be considered an underappreciated and unacknowledged trickle-down of troubles that occurs when ACVs get bumped to cover over-allowance costs, and why the practice shortchanges the possibility of achieving consistent profits when you wholesale and retail used vehicles.

Let's go back to the example of the vehicle an appraiser values a customer's trade-in at $15,000. A manager or sales associate presents this offer to the customer. You can see the customer's reaction. The offer isn't what the customer expects or wants for his/her vehicle. After some discussion, it becomes clear the customer will walk and not purchase a new vehicle if he/she can't get $16,500 for the trade-in.

This marks a critical moment of truth, or half-truth, for the vehicle's ACV. The manager and sales associate face a choice of whether to give the customer $16,500 or lose the new car deal, and the trade-in.

The manager will likely consider how badly the new vehicle department or the sales associate needs to make the deal. If it's almost the end of a month or a quarter, and the new vehicle sale will push the store closer to achieving its factory-set sales volume target, the manager may well decide to step up to satisfy the customer and get the new car deal.

If the manager approves the over-allowance to satisfy the customer, the next step is deciding how to account for the additional $1,500 cost in the deal. There are two typical paths dealers and managers follow in this moment.

The first path involves splitting the $1,500 over-allowance between the new car and the used car. In this instance, a manager might discount the new vehicle by $1,000 and bump the ACV by $500. The customer would see a total allowance of $16,500 for his/her vehicle on the new car deal sheet. The customer's happy. He/she got the money they wanted for the vehicle.

A similar scenario would involve adjusting or bumping the ACV for the full $1,500 cost of the over-allowance. The manager would change the $15,000 value the appraiser put on the vehicle to $16,500. Once again, the customer would see that the dealership would pay $16,500 for their trade-in—exactly the number they wanted.

In either scenario, the manager and sales associate are heroes in the eyes of the customer. They did what they had to do to satisfy the customer's trade-in value expectation. The customer got all the money, and the new car department puts another deal on the board.

But the decision to bump the ACV by either $500 or $1,500 creates a problem for the used vehicle department. The trade-in now carries a half-truth—the ACV no longer represents a true wholesale value, or the actual cash value the dealer could get for the vehicle if they sold it right away. Instead, the Adjusted Cash Value of $15,500 or $16,500, depending on the path the manager chose, creates a vehicle that carries an additional cost burden.

You can bet that, in this moment, the new vehicle manager isn't thinking about the used car department's new problem. For the manager and the sales associate, the trade-in is now a distant memory. The matter at hand, for them, is celebrating another new car deal that showed a decent-size gross profit from which they'll both get paid. They may even be high-fiving each other, depending on how much gross profit they were able to put on the books for the new car deal.

The most pressing decision in this moment of half-truth for the used vehicle and its ACV is exactly how the used vehicle manager decides to "get out" of the vehicle. The manager's primary concern is figuring out how best to dispatch the vehicle to show a satisfactory profit.

The manager would likely know, if they decide to wholesale the vehicle, that it won't get the $15,500 or $16,500 that shows as the car's ACV. In the wholesale market, buyers probably understand, just like the appraiser, that it's a $15,000 car. The manager is likely to face an immediate loss if the car goes to a wholesale buyer or auction.

The prospect of a wholesale loss may push the manager to retail the vehicle, irrespective of whether the used vehicle inventory needs it. Inevitably, the manager feels pressure to ensure the vehicle produces a positive front-end gross profit, even with the additional $500 or $1,500 cost. If the manager aims to make a $1,500 front-end gross profit, the vehicle may get listed in the retail market for $17,000 or $18,000—or even higher if the vehicle requires additional costs for reconditioning.

Unfortunately, as most readers should know, this strategy of trying to make up the cost of over-paying for a vehicle from a retail customer doesn't work as well as it used to, if at all. Used vehicle customers today are smart about what they should pay for their vehicle of choice. If the manager puts the car on the market to recover the $500 or $1,500 bump to its ACV, you can bet the vehicle won't garner as much interest from potential buyers as similar available vehicles that aren't burdened with this additional cost. In turn, the vehicle is likely to age in inventory until the manager reduces the asking price to reflect the actual retail value of the vehicle. When the vehicle finally sells, I think we can all agree that it will generate less front-end gross than it would have if it hit the front line with a more honest ACV and a more market-realistic retail price.

Such are the trickle-down problems created by bumping the ACV to cover the cost of trade-in over-allowances. The car's cost doesn't reflect a realistic wholesale value; it's a manager-adjusted or -preferred number. The car's eventual retail asking price isn't true to the market; it's a prayer, plain and simple. Perhaps the only real truths in the story of the vehicle with the ACV someone bumped by $500 or $1,500 is the suboptimal outcome the retail or wholesale sale produces—and the distrust and resentment the used vehicle manager brings to work every day.

Commissions Based on False Profits

But there's another half-truth that deserves greater attention. This half-truth rarely gets much notice or thought by anyone in the dealership. The half-truth is that, after bumping the ACV on the trade-in, the new vehicle department put a false profit on the books and paid generous commissions based on this false profit.

A MORE TRUTHFUL TERM FOR WHOLESALE VEHICLE VALUES

If a vehicle's Actual Cash Value (ACV) often represents a half-truth about a vehicle's value in the wholesale market, I'd advocate that dealers and managers stop using the term. Instead, they should consider a different, more truthful descriptor for a vehicle's wholesale value.

Consider the Baseline Wholesale Value, or BWV, from Project Upside.

The BWV is more representative of a vehicle's value in the wholesale market than third-party valuations since it's determined by accounting for specific characteristics and features of the vehicle itself. It's not a high-level roll-up of the transaction values of multiple vehicles.

I also like BWV because it more accurately reflects the reality of any vehicle you appraise and assess to figure out how much it's worth—until you actually sell the vehicle, you've only got a baseline for its eventual purchase in the wholesale market. With a truer view of a vehicle's BWV, dealers would have a better starting place to understand the minimum a

Except for a few used vehicle managers, no one will remember, when the trade-in sells as a retail unit and loses money, why the vehicle was effectively doomed to fail in the first place. No one connects the decision to bump the ACV by $500 or $1,500 to the vehicle's subsequent retail or wholesale loss, which often comes 30, 45, or even 60 days later.

I can understand why no one wants to connect the dots. The team in the new vehicle department wouldn't necessarily want anyone to know, or remember, that they were paid a generous commission on false profits for a new vehicle deal that should have been booked as a loss.

vehicle might achieve when it sells in the wholesale market, even if they choose not to use Bluebird to help them achieve the vehicle's best wholesale price.

With the BWV for a vehicle, dealers and managers might stop believing or pretending that the value of a vehicle they've adjusted or bumped to account for a trade-in over-allowance, or some other aspect of making a deal, represents the actual cash value of the vehicle.

In this way, the BWV could help usher in an era of more honesty and realism about the wholesale values of vehicles dealers choose to own—a first step toward understanding the whole truth of every wholesale vehicle and the best way to manage it.

It is for all these reasons that I'm advocating for more honesty with ACVs—if not abolishing the term altogether (see sidebar, this page). They should reflect the actual wholesale value of the vehicle, not the costs of completing new car deals. ACVs should not be bumped to help the new car department book false and phantom profits, from which they pay commissions. I also believe dealers would be in a better place if the profits and losses they booked in their new and used vehicle departments were real and true, rather than the summation of half-truths that occur every day.

I understand why these half-truths are so common. Until now, there really hasn't been a good reason or way to reckon with the costs and lost profit that follow decisions to over-allow and bump the ACVs on trade-ins. Why? Because there hasn't ever been a way to put a baseline wholesale value on a vehicle that truly represents an actual cash value the dealer might receive in the wholesale market.

This is where Project Upside enters the picture. For the first time in history, Project Upside will give dealers and managers a baseline wholesale value for a vehicle that means something. They'll have a wholesale value that corresponds to the cash you'd get for the car, plus a guaranteed minimum profit of $300 with potentially much more to come.

As I noted earlier in the chapter, Project Upside doesn't mean that you can't over-allow for trade-ins to make deals that are right and necessary for the new vehicle department. But if you bump the ACV to cover all or part of the over-allowance, you've effectively created a vehicle that loses its ability to generate the retail or whole-sale profit it might achieve if it wasn't burdened by the additional cost. In this way, the practice of bumping ACV can create subopti-mal outcomes for both the retail and wholesale barrels of business in every used vehicle department.

I believe the time has come for a different way of handling the cost of over-allowances—a more honest, truthful approach that allows you to continue to over-allow on trade-ins without crimp-ing the profit-producing potential of your used vehicle department and the double barrels of business it should be seeking to optimize.

CHAPTER 20

A CASE FOR ALLOCATING OVER-ALLOWANCES TO NEW CARS

I know that my call for dealers to stop bumping the Actual Cash Value (ACV) on trade-ins to account for trade-in over-allowances and make new vehicle deals seems like sacrilege to some.

I suspect everyone working in dealerships today has been taught that it's right and proper to bump the ACV and effectively charge the cost of the over-allowance to the used vehicle. It's how new car deals get done, and have been done, for the past 100 years of the car business.

Why would you want to do it any differently?

Let's answer this question with a quick examination of why the practice came to be in the first place.

I'd submit that the primary reason dealers began to use ACVs to account for trade-in over-allowances is that they could get away with it. Back in the day, no one knew any better. It wasn't possible for a used vehicle buyer to get a prevailing market price, or a fair market price, on a used car without a lot of work. Dealers could bump the ACV by $500, $1,000, $2,000, or even more and someone would pay it.

Today, consumers know better. This is why, when a vehicle's ACV gets bumped to cover the cost of a trade-in over-allowance and a manager prices the car to recover the cost, it often doesn't sell until someone puts the asking price where it should be.

Another reason bumping ACVs has become such a prevalent practice is that dealers have long considered their new vehicle department as the No. 1 priority for their dealerships. For nearly the past 100 years, the new vehicle departments at franchise dealerships have sold more cars and generated more total sales dollars and gross profit than the used vehicle department. As such, the new vehicle department gained primacy over the used vehicle department.

But even this long-standing reality has changed. In 2019, according to NADA dealership financial data, the new vehicle department generated 24.6 percent of the total gross profit the dealership generated; the used vehicle department, for the first time in history as far as I know, surpassed the new vehicle department by generating 24.8 percent of the dealership's total gross profit.

In 2020, a year in which all business performance might be considered suspect due to the COVID-19 pandemic, the new and used vehicle departments matched each other's contribution to the average dealership's total gross profit at 26.9 percent.

It's also worth noting that since 2016, the average number of new vehicles dealers retailed has been declining. Dealers sold 928 new vehicles in 2016, a figure that diminished to 866 in 2019.

Meanwhile, according to NADA, the volume of used vehicles retailed by franchise dealers has grown every year since 2009. To be sure, the sales pace of new and used vehicles for dealers in 2020 was off compared to prior years. NADA data for 2020 says new vehicle sales were down 10.7 percent compared to 2019, while used vehicle sales diminished 4.4 percent for the same year-over-year time period.

A Call New/Used Car Equality

My point and purpose in sharing this new and used vehicle performance data is to make the case that today's retail realities suggest that the used vehicle department should no longer play second fiddle or be subservient to the new vehicle department. The two departments should have equal footing, particularly when it comes to the practice of bumping ACVs to account for over-allowances on trade-ins that result from new vehicle deals. As I noted in the previous chapter, this practice creates a litany of problems—the used vehicle department can't optimize the profit on the vehicle, the new car department pays bonuses and commissions based on false profits, and no one recognizes the used vehicle's eventual retail or wholesale loss as a byproduct of the initial decision to bump the ACV.

I realize that eliminating the practice of charging the cost of over-allowances to used vehicles represents a significant shift in culture and perspective for many dealers. In fact, for some, it may well be a hill that's too steep to climb.

After all, once you start properly accounting for the costs of over-allowances, and book them against the new vehicle deal, the profitability of the new vehicle department will look worse than it may already be. Some dealers may lose their bragging rights in 20 Groups and make meetings. Suddenly, their financial composites will suggest they are underperforming their peers in new vehicle profitability.

"Hey, Bob," a 20 Group dealer might say. "What happened? Holy smokes, your new car department seems to lagging the rest of us."

If this occurs, I'd suggest that dealer Bob point out other parts of the financial composite that will shine brighter than his peers' after choosing to be honest and truthful about accounting for trade-in over-allowances. For one thing, Bob's used vehicle department sales and profitability will increase. Retail sales and profits will improve as managers stop trying to make up for the added costs of bumping ACVs to account for over-allowances. In addition, if Bob uses Project Upside, his wholesale profit loss/line will now show a consistent stream of steady profits. And, best of all, Bob's net profits for the dealership will look substantially better.

Some dealers might also resist the proper allocation of over-allowances to new vehicles out of fear that it will harm the high-flying performance and profits of their Finance and Insurance (F&I) departments. To be sure, new vehicles do drive significantly more F&I revenues than used vehicles. In 2020, F&I penetration ran nearly 91 percent on new vehicle sales compared to 76 percent on used vehicle sales. The dollars produced from these sales are sizable—more than $1 million in new vehicles compared to about $816,000 in used vehicles.

But the practice of properly allocating the cost of over-allowances to new vehicles won't jeopardize new vehicle sales or related F&I production. It's merely a matter of proper accounting. This new way of operating doesn't mean you *can't or shouldn't* over-allow on trade-ins when it's necessary. There will always be customers who want more for their vehicles than what an appraiser using Project Upside would consider an appropriate wholesale value. There will be times when it makes the most sense, from both a customer acquisition and financial perspective, to give the customer what he/she wants for the vehicle *and* make the new car deal. (This last scenario holds especially true if the trade-in will be a retail unit, and you know you can pay more than its baseline wholesale value and still make a profit.)

The only real difference is how you allocate the cost of the over-allowance and how you reward your managers and sales associates, given you're now booking more accurate and true costs associated with completing the new vehicle deal.

Once dealers make the decision to stop bumping ACVs to handle over-allowances on trade-ins, they'll need to decide how they'll account for the cost of the over-allowance. In my view, there are three ways dealers could handle over-allowances that will help them avoid booking false profits on new vehicles and creating problematic half-truths for the trade-in vehicle once they own it.

The first approach is the most straightforward: You allocate the cost of the over-allowance to the new vehicle deal through a discount or some other means. You would justify this allocation of the over-allowance based on the truth of what it represents—the cost of making the new car deal.

A second approach could be allocating the cost of the over-allowance to the advertising and marketing budget of the new vehicle department. Why? Because when you over-allow on a trade-in, you're effectively buying—or acquiring—a customer. The purpose of every advertising or marketing campaign—and the dollars invested to support them—is to acquire a customer. Since over-allowances are essentially a means to acquire a customer, it seems to me that dealers could rightfully allocate the cost of over-allowances to their advertising and marketing budgets—an approach that might be more palatable to dealers who are proud of the front-end profits they currently show in their new vehicle department.

The third approach might be charging the cost of the over-allowance to the quarterly or annual volume-tied bonus payment you receive from the factory as part of stair-step and other incentive programs. This approach would reflect the fact that the over-allowance effectively moves you closer to earning the bonus payment. Hence, it's reasonable and rationale to charge the cost to the bonus payment itself. Of course, this approach carries the risk that, if you don't earn the bonus, your trade-in over-allowance costs would show up in the new vehicle financials.

If it were my decision, I'd put the cost of the over-allowance directly on the new car deal. Doing so would give me the clearest view of the true costs of making new car deals and give my used vehicle department more clarity and latitude to optimize the financial outcome of every vehicle, whether it ends up a retail or wholesale unit.

I'd do something else, too. I would work long and hard to improve my appraisal process so I'd have fewer instances when customers expected more for their vehicles than what Project Upside and my manager believed the vehicle is truly worth. I would likely adopt as many of the elements of the "active" appraisal in my dealership as possible, and I would look for a baseline wholesale valuation, like the one Project Upside offers, that I could confidently consider as the ACV for the vehicle. I know from my experiences working with vAuto dealers, that when a dealer's team consistently follows an "active" appraisal strategy, the need for over-allowing on trade-ins goes away almost entirely.

When I've shared the idea of eliminating the practice of bumping ACVs and allocating the cost of trade-in over-allowances to the new vehicle department, some have questioned how factories might regard this different way of doing business. The honest answer is that I'm not sure.

I don't think factories would necessarily care how dealers allocate the cost of trade-in over-allowances provided the dealer's new vehicle sales production doesn't suffer. Factories might raise an eyebrow when dealers, for the sake of building a second barrel of profit-producing business in their used vehicle department, start reporting losses on new vehicle sales. Factories might not appreciate the fact that this more honest way of accounting for the costs of acquiring a new vehicle customer could make the privilege of selling their vehicles a less profitable prospect.

But I would view the additional factory focus as a good thing. Perhaps it'll finally stir more serious conversations about how dealers should be compensated for new vehicle sales—and how dealers might account for the factory bonus and stair-step incentive money that often make the difference between a dealership showing a profit or a loss at the end of the year.

I hope this chapter helps some dealers at least reconsider, if not fully change, the way they handle trade-in over-allowances. As I've stated, if you're going to continue to bump ACVs and effectively charge these costs to used vehicles, you will not be able to build a consistent profit-producing barrel of business in the used vehicle department.

I know. New car pride runs deep and strong for many dealers. You may not be ready or willing to allocate any costs for trade-in over-allowances to your new vehicle department, the new car department's advertising account, or your factory bonus plans. You may fundamentally believe that the cost of trade-in over-allowances should be assigned to the ACV. While I may not agree with this perspective, I understand it.

I'd also encourage those who doubt this new approach to consider three ways that having a baseline wholesale value from Project Upside can help strengthen the retail barrel of your used vehicle department.

CHAPTER 21

THREE WAYS PROJECT UPSIDE STRENGTHENS RETAIL OPERATIONS

I t'd be a big miss if, while writing a book about how dealers can build a second barrel of profitable business in their used vehicle departments, I failed to mention how knowing a true baseline wholesale value for a vehicle can strengthen the department's retail business.

Best I can tell, there are three primary ways a guarantee of a profit and no risk for every wholesale vehicle helps optimize the retail side of a used vehicle department.

First, you'll keep the right cars for the right reasons. Dealers and managers rightly regard themselves as retailers. They'll often talk about how they are "retail-first"—a phrase that points to their desire to retail every vehicle they can while regarding wholesale disposition of a vehicle as a last resort, if not a management failure. In recent years, though, I'd submit that the retail-first mindset has morphed into "retail-only," wherein dealers will attempt to retail just about any vehicle that isn't an obvious wholesale unit due to its condition, mileage, or some other factor. The retail-only mind-set can result in dealers and managers attempting to retail vehicles that, had they known a baseline wholesale value from Project Upside and its promise of a guaranteed minimum profit of $300 and potentially much more, they might have been better off selling as wholesale units.

Today, it's still common for roughly a third of all distressed or over-age vehicles in a dealer's inventory to have resulted from trade-ins. These investment-troubled units might represent a vehicle that came in off-lease and the dealer felt compelled by factory require-ments to own it, even though he/she had plenty of the same/similar vehicles in inventory. The trade-ins could be units that, for what-ever reason, weren't quite right for the dealer's retail inventory and market. They could be vehicles that ran into unexpected recondi-tioning costs that prompted a manager to put them on the market for too much money.

I'm not necessarily suggesting that these scenarios represented a bad decision or mistake. But I do believe that, at the time of a decision to keep or wholesale a vehicle, dealers and managers will be in a much better place when they know exactly what a decision to wholesale the vehicle might produce from an investment/mon-ey-making perspective—the exact insights that Project Upside and its money-making model are intended to provide.

If, for example, a manager understood that his/her retail inven-tory didn't need a recent customer trade, the manager could do the math to understand if a wholesale exit through Project Upside, as compared to the vehicle's retail prospects alongside the same/

similar vehicles already in inventory, made the most sense for the dealer's investment. This assessment or calculation isn't possible today because dealers and managers haven't had a way to know with any degree of certainty what a vehicle's wholesale exit might look like.

On the other side, if a manager needs a vehicle for his/her retail inventory, Project Upside's appraisal process will ensure a clearer understanding of the vehicle's condition and provide a better baseline to perform the retail-back calculation to determine how much to pay the customer for the vehicle and set its initial retail asking price.

Whatever the specific set of circumstances surrounding a vehicle, Project Upside helps dealers and managers make a better-informed decision about the best exit strategy—retail or wholesale—for a vehicle.

Ultimately, Project Upside will help dealers sharpen their retail-first focus and avoid the trap of unknowingly becoming retail-only operators who too often take in cars for the wrong costs and the wrong reasons. Project Upside may even bring a day when distressed and over-age units that came from trade-ins will be a thing of the past.

Second, you'll pay the right money for trade-ins. With a more accurate and relevant baseline wholesale value in hand from Project Upside; a pencil-sharp estimate of reconditioning costs; and a clearer, whole-truth approach to accounting for the cost of over-allowing on trade-ins, dealers and managers will be better able to ensure that they're taking in trade-ins for the right money. In turn, used vehicle managers will no longer feel a need to price vehicles to make up the cost of overvaluing a trade-in due to an over-allowance, an uncertain view of the vehicle's reconditioning costs, or a lack of certainty about its baseline wholesale value. With more market-realistic and -relevant numbers from the get-go, a larger share of the trade-ins you retail will sell while their gross profit potential is the greatest and hasn't run out—a fact that sales associates will appreciate as they're walking customers to these cars.

Finally, you'll be better positioned to acquire more inventory from customers. As the costs of acquiring auction inventory have increased in recent years, and with the unprecedented wholesale value appreciation that has occurred in 2020 and 2021, more dealers and managers have implemented strategies to acquire more vehicles directly from customers. Such efforts offer the prospect of acquiring inventory on a more cost- and profit-favorable basis. In some cases, particularly when customers share that they plan to purchase a vehicle when they get out of their current vehicle, dealers receive the added benefit of a retail deal.

But I've found many of the "we'll buy your car" efforts only find limited success. Why? The main reason, I believe, is that dealers and managers tend to apply a "retail-only" eye to the cars customers bring to their attention. If a customer doesn't have a vehicle the dealer or manager believes he/she can retail, no one shows any interest in the customer. You can see evidence of this problem in the backlog of unaddressed or unanswered leads from services like Kelley Blue Book's Instant Cash Offer. Even though a customer has raised a hand, no one followed up because the vehicle doesn't meet the used vehicle department's retail parameters or strategy.

With Project Upside, dealers and managers who tend to cherry-pick these acquisition opportunities would have greater incentive to contact these customers and at least engage them about their vehicle. The dealers and managers would know that if they acquired a vehicle and it needed to get wholesaled, they would get a guaranteed minimum profit of $300 and potentially much more. They would be less likely to view the customer's vehicle as a piece of "trash" they'd prefer to ignore.

Project Upside can also change the way dealers and managers view acquiring vehicles from customers. It shifts from a bother and a burden to a more consistent and reliable source of profit-making used vehicle inventory. It won't matter if you're acquiring cars you know you'll wholesale—because you'll also know they'll make money with Project Upside. And, if the cars you acquire do fit your retail inventory needs, you know you brought them in for the right money, for the right reasons.

It's a win-win scenario, with one exception—the wholesalers who may have depended on you for the cars you acquired from customers and decided to wholesale. They will continue to come around, and they will continue to make offers on your cars. In this way, they may even represent a temptation to go for quick money on specific vehicles. In the next chapter, I'll attempt to explain why I believe it's best that dealers resist the temptation and the suboptimal outcomes that are sure to follow.

CHAPTER 22

RESISTING TEMPTATION FOR QUICK WHOLESALE PROFITS

There's at least one individual, and perhaps more than one, who will not appreciate a dealership's decision to use Project Upside to build a double-barreled business in the used vehicle department.

This individual would be the wholesale buyer who has become accustomed to acquiring the vehicles you take in on trade and plan to wholesale. As we've discussed earlier, wholesale buyers aren't working for charity. Just like dealers, wholesale buyers are in the business of making money. They extract their profit from the margin they negotiate between the purchase price for a dealer's wholesale vehicle or package of vehicles and the sales price(s) they expect to achieve in the wholesale market.

It's this money-making opportunity that effectively goes away for wholesale buyers when dealers and managers opt to use Project

Upside to wholesale all the trade-ins they take in and don't plan to retail, thus earning a guaranteed minimum profit with no risk.

You can bet wholesale buyers will take notice when the supply of available vehicles from a dealer goes away as Project Upside enters the picture. This change may even spur some wholesale buyers to work harder to convince a dealer or manager that the purchase price they're offering right here, and right now, would produce a better financial outcome than if the dealer wholesales a vehicle through Project Upside.

Even though dealers and managers who use Project Upside are expected to use the system to wholesale all of the trade-ins they don't retail, you can bet they will be tempted to take the wholesaler's money, especially if it means booking a profit on a vehicle today that's larger than the minimum of $300 in profit that Project Upside will guarantee on a vehicle. It will be tempting for dealers to say "yes" in this critical moment, without recognizing that they might be making a suboptimal financial decision on the vehicle.

Let's tease out how this temptation might transpire. To do so, we'll go back to the trade-in vehicle that has a Project Upside baseline wholesale value of $15,000. If the dealer or manager uses the system to sell the vehicle, they would see a minimum of $300 in guaranteed profit, plus the opportunity to make more profit when Project Upside sells the vehicle to achieve its best wholesale price.

That's when the wholesaler might say, "I'll give you $16,000 for the car—$700 more than the guarantee you'll get from Project Upside. Even better, I'll give you the money today."

If a wholesale buyer makes this offer on the vehicle, you know two things are true—the buyer is in the business of making money, and he/she also believes they'll get more than $16,000 for the vehicle when it sells in the wholesale market.

It's at this moment that a dealer or used vehicle manager may say "yes" to the wholesaler's offer. The thinking might go something like this: "$1,000 right now is better than $300. There's no guarantee that Project Upside would pay me more than $300 and, even if Project Upside pays me 90 percent of the upside it sees, I still might not make the $1,000 I can get today."

On one hand, you can't fault the dealer or manager for wanting to take the $1,000 right away. It'd provide immediate gratification and more gross profit than the dealership sometimes sees with retail sales of used vehicles.

But on the other hand, the decision to take the $1,000 would overlook another reality about the wholesaler's offer. It can't and doesn't reflect what the best wholesale price of the vehicle might be in the wholesale market. After all, as we've discussed in prior chapters, one can only find the best wholesale price for a vehicle when the car is presented in accord with the wholesale playbook—in a setting where there's a curated critical quantity of cars and highly motivated buyers, and the vehicle is offered in a transparent manner and put up for sale with the full intention of selling it the first time it runs.

In our example, the wholesaler's offer represents what a single buyer might pay. If a manager says "yes" to the offer, he/she is effectively saying the offer is the best the vehicle can achieve, which simply isn't true in this moment. The decision would ignore or look past the very real possibility that Project Upside is likely to sell the vehicle on the dealer's behalf for more than $16,000 and share

90 percent of the upside with the dealer. If Project Upside sells the car for $16,500, for example, the dealer's total profit would be $1,380 (the initial $300 minimum guarantee plus 90 percent of the $1,200 upside, or $1,080).

In addition, the manager would be falling for the same temptation that can create suboptimal outcomes with financial investments. We've all felt the temptation to pull money out of index funds to chase what seems like a can't-miss, quick-return investment opportunity. When these moments arise for me, it helps to talk with my more-astute financial friends, who will remind me of the reliable law of averages that spurred me to put my investment money in index funds like Vanguard. The advisors will note that if you go after the short-term return, you're undermining the strategy of meeting or beating market returns over the long term.

Such wisdom may not resonate with a dealer or manager in this moment of temptation. The wholesaler's offer of $1,000 profit right away may be too rich to pass up.

But beyond the temptation, the offer also represents a test. For dealers and managers in this critical decision-making moment, when a wholesaler's flashing cash, it's a test of your commitment and resolve to use Project Upside to build a second barrel of consistent, profit-producing business in your used vehicle department.

Before I share how pointers to help dealers and managers prepare to build their double-barreled business opportunity and resist the temptation of the wholesaler's offer, I need to highlight another temptation that comes wrapped in the promise of an "Easy" button for selling wholesale vehicles.

CHAPTER 23

BEWARE OF THE BIG RED "EASY" BUTTON

I n early 2005, the office supply chain Staples debuted its "Easy" button ads. Some readers may remember them. The ads were funny. They would feature difficult situations like a student unable to answer a teacher's question about the value of "N" in a math equation, a doctor prepping for a surgery he'd never performed before, or a father trying to change diapers on twins.

The actors would press a big red "Easy" button, and Boom! The problem goes away.

While the ads, and the ubiquity of Staples stores in shopping centers across America, have been long gone, you still hear people joking about having an "Easy" button when faced with difficult circumstances.

The "Easy" button ads from Staples come to mind as I regard the remarkable rise in recent years of companies and solutions that pitch dealers and managers on an easier, more convenient, and more transparent way to buy and sell wholesale vehicles. The digital auction companies also promote their services as far cheaper than traditional auction outlets due to lower fees for buyers and sellers.

The companies tout an almost care- and worry-free whole-sale-selling experience. It's like pressing an "Easy" button. You hand the keys to a rep, and your work is done.

With the services, the cars don't leave your lot. The cars get inspected. The details of listing the cars, with condition reports and photos, are handled. The cars go up for sale on a company-managed auction platform. If your vehicles sell, you purportedly pay less in fees and save money.

You can bet some dealers and managers love these solutions. They seem like a godsend. Dealers and managers don't have to deal with wholesalers who regularly visit the used vehicle department looking for cars. The companies relieve the hassle and time associated with sending cars to an auction and managing the sales.

Now, to be clear, I'm not referring to the "Easy"-button-like solutions offered by traditional auction companies. For example, Cox Automotive offers Manheim Express Concierge, a service that helps dealers inspect, list, and sell wholesale vehicles in Manheim's online marketplaces. While the solution shares convenience-minded services the digital-only auction companies offer to help dealers wholesale vehicles, there is also a distinct difference. The difference is that, in the case of Manheim Express, the service is tied to a company that has long provided online and physical auctions where critical quantities of vehicles and buyers routinely converge.

Therein lies my concern that the nascent, digital-only auction companies aren't as cheap for dealers as the companies contend. In fact, I'd make the case that when dealers sell vehicles through these digital auctions, they cost more—and deliver less—than dealers and managers believe.

Consider, for example, the size of the individual marketplaces the digital-only auction companies manage. The number of cars and buyers represented in these companies' auction spaces is anemic compared to the critical quantities that converge at digital auctions run by larger auction companies. None of the digital-only companies has yet to build a critical quantity of cars and buyers that would enable them to achieve best wholesale prices.

The critical quantity problem gets compounded when you consider how at least one of the companies promises that vehicles will sell in minutes, not a matter of days. This approach works well if you regard your wholesale vehicles as trash that needs a quick disposal. It works less effectively when you realize that a smaller number of cars are coming and going fast in front of a small pool of buyers. I question whether the "Jerry Springer (anything can happen)" effect can take hold and sellers can maximize value in such short windows of time.

I also question whether the smaller-scale digital settings do anything to address the first-run sales efficiency problem that has long plagued the way dealers and managers sell vehicles in the wholesale market. From what I understand, dealers and managers do not achieve first-run sales efficiency rates any better than they do in more traditional auction settings, and often less. Why? The first reason is that the smaller-scale digital auctions aren't curating the cars to ensure optimal outcomes for dealers; they're running them as they arrive, which isn't as friendly to buyers as it could or should be. The second reason isn't necessarily the fault of the digital auction providers themselves; it mostly owes, I believe, to unrealistic floors that sellers expect for their vehicles.

We also see a curious trajectory for vehicles that dealers sell in the smaller-scale digital auctions. The vehicles will leave the digital auction setting and reappear, almost overnight, in the online and physical sales offered by larger auctions.

The cars aren't resurfacing in other auctions because sellers pulled them out of the digital auction and took them somewhere else. No, the cars resurface because a wholesale buyer found an opportunity to extract value from the smaller-scale digital auction (and by extension the selling dealer) and make a profit in the larger auction setting, where there is a greater opportunity for critical quantity and best wholesale prices.

When the team and I began building Project Upside, we realized that the car business doesn't need another online auction—it needs a better way for dealers and managers to conduct their wholesale business that assures a profit and feeds their retail success.

To be sure, Project Upside does not represent an "Easy" button, but it does promise more optimal, money-making outcomes for dealers who use it.

Project Upside requires dealers and managers to ensure they capture as much information about a vehicle's condition as possible to inspire the confidence in buyers that leads to best wholesale prices when the vehicles sell. It forces a rethinking of what the actual cash value (ACV) of a vehicle should represent and of how to handle over-allowances on trade-ins so neither barrel of profit-producing business in the used vehicle department suffers. In exchange for this effort, Project Upside is able to guarantee a minimum profit of $300 for every wholesale vehicle dealers and managers choose to sell through the system, plus 90 percent of any upside if the vehicle sells for more than the cost of the vehicle and the minimum $300 profit.

Time will tell if our vision for Project Upside offers sufficient appeal to dealers and managers that they'll choose to wholesale their vehicles in the new way the system offers. Of course, we believe the Project Upside way is the better way, and we've invested significant resources and time to create and offer this market-transformative solution to dealers.

Throughout the book, I've tried to paint the picture that building a second barrel of profit-producing business in your used vehicle department is within reach with Project Upside. But achieving the outcome of consistent wholesale profits requires far more than pressing an "Easy" button. It will require a commitment, on the part of dealers and managers, to move away from considering their wholesale vehicles as "trash" and recognize, like top-performing wholesale sellers like CarMax and Carvana, that these cars do, in fact, represent a profit-making treasure if they're handled correctly.

I have some thoughts on how dealers and managers can begin to embrace the new, better way forward that Project Upside offers. They're spelled out in the next chapter.

CHAPTER 24

BUILDING YOUR DOUBLE-BARRELED USED VEHICLE SUCCESS

I would imagine that everyone reading this book has a smart phone. Chances are that phone is probably within arm's reach, even as you're reading right now.

Take a moment to pick up the phone and give it a good look. Now, ask yourself: "When is the last time you received a prompt and hit 'OK,' to update the phone's operating system?"

My guess is that the most recent update occurred in the last few weeks, if not days. Such is the nature of technology these days. It changes fast and, as end users, we are then pushed to update our phones and get used to a new operating system and, sometimes, a new way of doing things.

Now, let's ask another question: "When's the last time you did anything different with the way you manage the vehicles you whole-sale to buyers or at auctions?" I suspect the answer to this question is easier to answer than remembering the last time you updated your smartphone. Why? Because the way most dealers manage the wholesale business in their used vehicle departments hasn't changed much, if at all, from the days when guys with cowboy hats and pink Cadillacs came around to take the wholesale vehicles you didn't want off your hands.

The lack of significant change in the way dealers manage and sell wholesale vehicles stands in stark contrast to all the changes that have occurred in the car business in the past 20 years, and especially the past five years.

Today, nearly every dealer operates their used vehicle department with an inventory management system. These systems didn't exist prior to the arrival of the Internet and the higher level of market efficiency and transparency it brought to the used vehicle business.

Think of your inventory acquisition and how much it's changed. It used to be common for used vehicle managers and buyers to spend the bulk of their work weeks traveling to auctions to acquire inventory. Today, and especially in light of the effective shutdown of physical auctions amid the COVID-19 pandemic in 2020, used vehicle managers rarely, if ever, set foot in a physical auction to acquire inventory. They use technology and tools to find, appraise, and purchase the auction vehicles they need.

Consider how you desk deals. While it's not uncommon for dealers to negotiate the purchase price of used vehicles, the fact is that, for many dealers, the end result is essentially a "near one-price" approach. That is, you're using the fact that you know, and the customer knows, that you've priced your used vehicles competitively—and any haggling amounts to a few hundred dollars. In addition, it's increasingly the case that the negotiation doesn't happen at a physical desk; it occurs in the engagement that precedes a customer's visit to the showroom, often between your sales associates or BDC team members.

The way dealers price their retail inventory is changing dramatically, too. Some dealers now put their trust in technology and tools, rather than the wisdom of a manager, to know exactly where to price a used vehicle based on its investment value. Retail asking prices for used vehicles still reflect the manager's discretion and judgment, but the time required to determine the right price for a used vehicle is a matter of seconds, not minutes.

To be sure, some dealers have sought to improve the way they manage and sell wholesale vehicles. In the past few years, we've seen the rise of more digital marketplaces that promise a more cost-effective and efficient way to liquidate the vehicles you take in on trade and choose not to retail.

But, by and large, the rise of these new auctions doesn't change the fundamental inefficiencies that currently hinder a dealer's ability to build a double-barreled business in their used vehicle department—the cars go for sale with half-truths about their condition and actual cash values; the selling dealers still carry all the risk; and, because none of these entities have yet to build a critical quantity of cars and buyers, they aren't really bringing the full power of the wholesale playbook to work on behalf of dealers who bring the cars.

Therein lies the fundamental difference with Project Upside. It offers dealers the opportunity to harness the full profit-making power of the wholesale playbook for themselves. Even better, as I've tried to underscore throughout the book, Project Upside isn't just about improving wholesale outcomes for dealers. Its benefits help dealers become better, more profitable retailers, too.

It'd be nice if bringing Project Upside into your dealership would be as easy as turning on the system, like you do when you update your smartphone. Unfortunately, it won't be that easy.

Dealers and managers will need to be the stewards of a significant shift in the belief systems and cultures that are nearly universal across used vehicle departments. You must believe that you deserve to make money when you wholesale vehicles. You must believe that you will make money as Project Upside ensures you achieve the Rule of 200 month in and month out. You must believe that the solution's index fund-based model will produce better outcomes than individual managers who pick and choose their wholesaling opportunities. You must believe that it's in your best interests—and your customer's best interest—to appraise and value every trade-in opportunity on the merits of the vehicle's condition and mileage and through a two-way engagement with each customer that builds mutual respect and trust. You have to believe that the best outcome of your trade-in process isn't stealing a car from a customer—it's bringing in the car at a purchase price that's a good decision for them, and for you, irrespective of its retail or wholesale exit strategy.

The responsibility for bringing this new belief system—and the culture it will create and foster in your new and used vehicle departments—will ultimately rest with dealers and managers. It'll be on them to lead their teams to not only adopt a different way of doing business but to believe, in the fullness of their hearts, that the new way is the best way forward, with everyone involved, including themselves.

Dealers and managers will face doubt, and even outright resistance, as they lead their teams toward building a double barrel of profit-producing business in the used vehicle department. The transition will inevitably bring its share of personal and professional tests. In these moments, I would encourage dealers and managers to remember the leadership they are paid to provide. The job isn't about doing things right—it's about doing the right things.

I believe Project Upside is right for dealers, right now and for the future. It represents an unprecedented opportunity to operate with the whole truth of wholesaling in mind and to make money from investments dealers have long regarded as losers.

Project Upside represents a big step, even bigger than updating your smartphone. That's why I stand ready to help you take it.

ABOUT THE AUTHOR

DALE POLLAK'S career in the automotive industry spans more than two decades. As a dealer, technology entrepreneur, and best-selling author, Pollak has helped over 10,000 automotive dealers in North America make dramatic improvements in their new and used vehicle operations.

Pollak pioneered the Velocity Method of Management™. It maximizes a dealer's profitability through the use of new and used vehicle market metrics. Pollak crafted this approach during his years as a Cadillac dealer in Chicago in light of his unique circumstances of not being able to physically observe his used vehicle inventory due to blindness.

His investment and market-based approach served as the foundation for vAuto, Inc., the company that he founded in 2005. Since then, the company's technology and tools have been adopted by thousands of dealerships in North America. In late 2010, AutoTrader.com acquired vAuto, with both companies now operating as a part of the Cox Automotive family. Pollak continues to guide strategic product development/integration for vAuto and other Cox Automotive companies. Prior to vAuto, Pollak helped build and lead Digital Motorworks, Inc., to its successful acquisition in 2002.

Pollak has written three books that detail the application of the Velocity Method of Management™ in dealerships. The latest, *Velocity Overdrive: The Road to Reinvention*, was released in 2012. His most recent book, *Gross Deception: Shifting Markets, Shrinking Margins and the New Truth of Used Car Profitability*, was released in February 2020.

Pollak holds a BS in Business Administration from Indiana University, a law degree from DePaul University's College of Law, and is a four-time winner of the American Jurisprudence Award. In addition, Pollak received the 2010 Ernst and Young Entrepreneur of the Year Award, and in 2011, Pollak was inducted into the Chicago Area Entrepreneurship Hall of Fame. In 2014, Pollak was named as Poling Chair at the Indiana University Kelley School of Business. He also currently serves as a transportation advisor to the Federal Reserve Bank of Chicago.